CORE FITNESS

FITNESS FOR THE MIND AND BODY

CORE FITNESS

HOLLIS LANCE LIEBMAN

ROSEN
PUBLISHING

New York

Published in 2015 by The Rosen Publishing Group, Inc.
29 East 21st Street, New York, NY 10010

© 2015 Hinkler Books

First Edition

Library of Congress Cataloging-in-Publication Data

Liebman, Hollis Lance.
Core fitness/Hollis Lance Liebman. — First Edition.
    pages cm. — ((Fitness for the Mind and Body))
Includes bibliographical references and index.
Audience: Grades: 7-12.
ISBN 978-1-4777-8168-5 (Library bound)
1. Exercise—Juvenile literature. 2. Muscle strength—Juvenile literature. I. Title.
GV481.L637 2015
613.7—dc23

                                                                2014023545

Manufactured in the United States of America

Always do the warm-up exercises before attempting any individual exercises. It is recommended that you check with your doctor or healthcare professional before commencing any exercise regime. While every care has been taken in the preparation of this material, the publishers and their respective employees or agents will not accept responsibility for injury or damage occasioned to any person as a result of participation in the activities described in this book.

Contents

Your core 8

Working out at home 14

Nourishing your core 16

Full-body anatomy 20

WARM-UPS

Supine Lower-Back Stretch 24

Side Stretch 25

Half-Kneeling Rotation 26

CORE STABILIZERS

Plank 30

Plank-Up 32

Side Plank 34

Side Plank with Reach-Under 36

Side Plank with Band Row 38

Fire-Hydrant In-Out 40

T-Stabilization 42

Fitness Ball Atomic Push-Up 44

Fitness Ball Pike 46

Fitness Ball Jackknife 48

Fitness Ball Lateral Roll 50

Fitness Ball Rollout 52

Fitness Ball Hyperextension 54

Mountain Climber 56

Body-Weight Squat 58

Medicine Ball Squat to Press 60

Balance Push-Up 62

Kneel on Ball 64

Medicine Ball Over-the-Shoulder Throw 66

Fitness Ball Split Squat 68

Fitness Ball Prone Row to External Rotation 70

Fitness Ball Seated External Rotation 72

Medicine Ball Walkover 74

Fitness Ball Band Fly 76

Fitness Ball Walk-Around 78
Medicine Ball Pullover on Fitness Ball 80
Side Lunge and Press 82
Hip Crossover 84
Hip Raise 86
Fitness Ball Hip Raise 88
Fitness Ball Bridge 90
Stiff-Legged Deadlift 92
Standing One-Legged Row 94

CORE STRENGTHENERS

Sit-Up 98
Rise and Reach 100
One-Armed Sit-Up 102
Medicine Ball Sit-Up 104
Crunch 106
Bicycle Crunch 108
Diagonal Crunch with Medicine Ball 110
Fitness Ball Side Crunch 112
V-Up 114
Fitness Ball Crunch 116
Reverse Crunch 118
Big Circles with Medicine Ball 120
Medicine Ball Slam 122
Kneeling Crunch with Band 124
One-Armed Band Pull 126
Penguin Crunch 128
Wood Chop with Band 130
Wood Chop with Fitness Ball 132
Medicine Ball Standing Russian Twist 134
Fitness Ball Seated Russian Twist 136
Fitness Ball Russian Twist 138
Fitness Ball Alternating Leg Tuck 140
Leg Raise 142

Side Leg Raise 144

Body Saw 146

Side Bend 148

Vertical Leg Crunch 150

Band Roll-Down with Twist 152

Good Mornings 154

Superman 156

COOL-DOWNS

Back Arch Stretch 160

Child's Pose 161

Fitness Ball Abdominal Stretch 162

WORKOUTS

Beginner's Workout 166

Over-Fifty Workout 166

Upper-Abdominal Workout 168

Lower-Abdominal Workout 168

Global Workout 170

Sports Workout 172

Warrior Workout 174

Beach-Bod Bikini Workout 176

Balance and Postural Workout 176

Power Workout 178

Conclusion 180

Glossary 182

Icon Index 186

About the Author/Credits 192

Your core

In the last decade, working the core has become all the rage. But core consciousness is no mere fad—awareness of the importance of a strong, stable core is the key to a stronger self.

These days, fitness enthusiasts invoke the word *core* so often that it can be hard to tell what it really means. Everyone from the new mother wanting to firm her midsection to the weekend tennis warrior seeking more power and accuracy in his backhand swing to the sedentary executive just looking to get through the day without lower-back pain seems to be talking about the core. And for anyone who wants improved posture, or simply to look slimmer and fitter, the idea of "working the core" holds great currency.

What is the core?
The core comprises a system of muscles in the lower-trunk area including the lower back, abdomen, and hips. These muscles work together to provide support and mobility, and it is through them that all bodily movement, in every conceivable direction, originates.

The major core muscles include the spinal flexors, spinal extensors, hip flexors, and hip extensors. The spinal flexors are also known as the anterior abdominals—the muscle group usually referred to as simply the abdominals or the "abs." The abdominal group consists of the rectus abdominis, transversus abdominis, and internal and external obliques. The rectus abdominis, commonly called the "six-pack," is responsible for maintaining spinal stability as well as shortening the distance between your torso and hips. The transversus abdominis provides thoracic and pelvic stability. Both the internal and external obliques are responsible for your ability to bend from side to side and rotate your torso.

The spinal extensors, also known as the posterior abdominals, include the erector spinae, quadratus lumborum, and multifidus spinae. The Christmas tree-shaped erector spinae is actually a group of muscles and tendons that stretches from the lumbar to the cervical spine. The erector spinae is responsible for stabilization as well as movement of your spine.

The hip flexors are the iliopsoas, rectus femoris, sartorius, tensor fasciae latae, pectineus, adductor longus, adductor brevis, and gracilis. The hip extensors include the gluteus maximus and the hamstrings, which are made up of the biceps femoris, semitendinosus, and semimembranosus. The hip flexors and extensors act as the basement of this muscular powerhouse, supporting movement and allowing you to flex and extend your hips.

A strong core is paramount to keeping your body functionally sound and operational. Many quick-fix diets, pieces of exercise equipment, and even surgeries promise a sleeker, better-looking abdominal area, but it is through core training that focuses on the strength and flexibility of these muscle groups—coupled with a healthful diet—that you can achieve real, long-lasting results.

A stronger core = a stronger body
Aside from the obvious aesthetic benefits of maintaining a lean and tight core, there are important functional pluses as well. Imagine easing back pain, improving your balance, standing straighter (and in the process, looking taller), and lifting heavy objects without stress or strain. A strong core allows you to execute everyday movements with ease, even as you age. Core training is an insurance policy for keeping the body performing at peak levels.

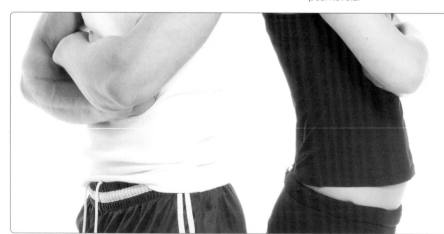

Good things in small packages
The core is the only muscle system in the body that we train for compactness— rather than for volume, as we tend to do for other muscle groups, such as those of the chest or arms. As you train your core, the ultimate goal is not only to have a sleek, toned midsection, but also to attain a functionally sound core that can rotate, contract, and support you whichever way you move.

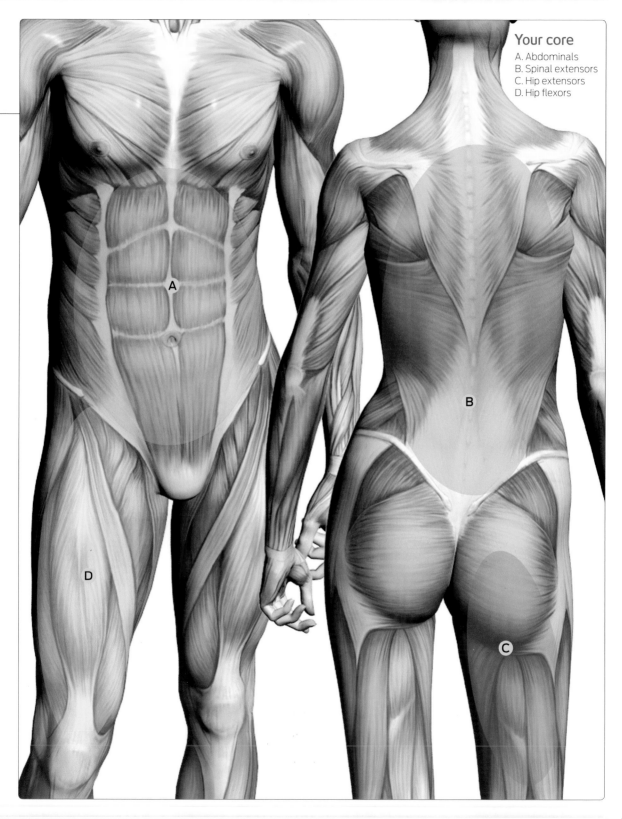

Your core

A. Abdominals
B. Spinal extensors
C. Hip extensors
D. Hip flexors

Maintaining a strong core will also lend optimal support to ancillary (assisting) muscles. In fact, the core is so central to your body's movement that it is called upon whenever any muscle in the body is used. Have you ever exercised your upper arms and discovered later that your midsection was quite sore? That was your core at work.

Your body's central power station

The core is constantly assisting other muscle groups as they function, acting as the fulcrum for all motion. When you squat down to pick up something from the floor, your core muscles work to maintain the integrity of vertical movement. And when you lift an object overhead you mainly recruit your deltoids and triceps, but your core muscles are also working to both support and balance you, keeping your torso steady as you lift. If your core muscles were not engaging, proper trunk alignment would be nearly impossible. That kind of motion, unassisted by the core, would be both much more difficult and potentially dangerous due to spinal compression.

The core acts as the central power station from which all muscular movement originates. Your ability to squat down to retrieve an object comes from the simultaneous firing of the quadriceps and gluteal muscles, with the core assisting by contracting and keeping the body in line. Whether you are working out or just carrying out your everyday tasks, attempting muscular contraction without aid from the core is like turning on the television without plugging it in.

Core-training basics

Core training is about treating the body as a unified whole. You may feel the effects of some of the exercises in this book in one region of your body more strongly than in others, but these workouts are designed to improve muscular function, strengthening, and stabilization throughout your entire body.

You draw upon your core muscles every day. Although rarely in daily life will you find yourself contracting your biceps or extending your arms to full lockout from your chest as if you're doing a bench press, it's not uncommon to lift an object off the ground and rotate your trunk in order to put it down. This movement is accomplished through reliance on

Put it in neutral

Neutral position, also known as neutral spine and neutral posture, is a key element of core training. You need to understand it before commencing a core-training regimen.

Neutral position is one of the most efficient positions from which to begin movement; it ensures that you properly target and strengthen your core muscles. While in neutral, your spine is in the proper alignment between postural extremes. In its natural alignment, your spine isn't straight—it curves at the neck, upper back, and lower back. These curves act as protection against spinal stress and strain.

Adjusting the tilt of your pelvis will also adjust the alignment of your spine. If you rotate your pelvis backward, you'll notice that the curve of your lower back increases; rotating it forward diminishes that curve.

To find your neutral position while lying on your back, place your thumbs on your hip bones and your fingers over your pubic bone (the bone between your legs), to create a triangle. In neutral position, all of the bones will line up on the same plane—neither tipping back nor shifting to one side.

To find neutral position while lying on your stomach, press your pubic bone into your exercise mat until you feel your back flatten slightly or your stomach lightly lift. Tuck your chin so that your forehead rests against your mat.

Challenge your core

Our widespread dependence on artificial support, such as chair backs that shoulder for us the work of sitting up straight, has left many of us with weak spines and soft middles. Imagine all of those hours spent slouching, without challenging your core, so that upon rising your back feels strained to the point of pain. If you have a sedentary job, you are likely to benefit greatly from challenging your core through exercise. You can also augment your fitness regimen with a simple addition to your work environment.

If you spend hours behind a desk, try replacing your office chair with a fitness ball. To maintain your balance while sitting on an unstable ball, you must make constant minute postural adjustments, which strongly engages your core. Some manufacturers are now producing specialized balance ball chairs.

not one isolated muscle, but rather on a group of muscles, including the core, working together.

The three keys to core fitness

The keys to successfully executing a core workout are breathing, form, and speed. With a firm command of these three elements, you can develop your core muscles efficiently and effectively. Endless repetitions are neither necessary nor advisable; you need only carry out a few calculated sets to achieve a deep muscular burn.

Breathing

Keep your breathing pace natural and steady. Couple a deep inhale with the negative, or stretching, of the muscle. Think of the inhalation as pulling back the arrow on an archer's bow before launch, and follow it with a deep exhale on the positive, or extended, portion of the movement   as if you were releasing the arrow. Aim for a

slow or controlled negative followed by an explosive positive and a slight hold at the peak contraction or finished position.

Form

Form is critical to effective core training. Every exercise has its proper starting position, movement path, and action. As you read through the steps to a new exercise, think about those three things, and take the time to properly execute each step with control and precision. Maintain that control through every repetition; controlled exercising develops strength, stamina, flexibility, and ease of movement.

Speed

Neither rush through your reps nor greatly slow them; instead, adopt a natural pace that you can sustain throughout the set while keeping proper form. It is human nature to avoid pain, which is why so many gym-goers perform excessive sets at a lowered intensity or with a limited range of motion. But a few focused and well-executed sets that focus on the muscle's full range and a peak contraction at the top will always be far more effective than too many go-through-the-motions sets.

Give your all during each and every rep performed. That guy at the gym who claims that he can do a thousand sit-ups would in reality be lucky to complete a hundred that truly work his core, because the neck and lower back—not to mention speed and momentum—usually do all the work when so many repetitions are involved. For best results, less is more: aim to lengthen the muscle, then contract and squeeze. Place the tension on the core muscles at hand without calling in recruits.

From warm-up to cool-down

Cold muscles are susceptible to strains, pulls, and tears, so before you begin any workout session, it's best to "thaw

out" your muscles. Your body performs optimally when it is warmed and primed for performance. Just 5 to 10 minutes of moderate cardiovascular work, such as pedaling a stationary bicycle or walking on a treadmill, followed by 5 minutes of stretching, warms up your body, preparing it for the rigorous demands you'll place upon it, and protecting it from injury. Stretching improves the flexibility in a given muscle and increases its range of motion, which promotes the development of lean muscle tissue. It also improves the rate and quality of your body's processing of nutrients.

Just as you should warm up before you begin your core-training workout, you should cool down after it. Exercise elevates your heart rate and loosens your muscles. A few minutes of stretching and cardio activity will effectively lower your heart rate and help to rid your body of lactic acid and other toxins created as by-products of your workout. Proper warm-ups and cool-downs help ensure long-term performance in and out of the gym.

Core stability and core strength

This book focuses on both core strength and core stability. Stability exercises work the muscles that support your core during motion. To stabilize is to both secure your spine and work your visible abdominal muscles. During the execution of a core-stabilizing exercise, your spine should remain in a neutral position without any movement. Stability exercises focus on improving your core functionality over defining your abdominal musculature.

Core-strengthening exercises work the core directly, building strength and endurance as well as muscles. These are the moves that can give you the "six-pack" abs look, in which each segment of the rectus abdominis is highly defined. Core-strengthening exercises generally target the rectus abdominis, the transversus abdominis, and the obliques. In the process, the muscles of your midsection become more compact, taking inches from your waistline.

How to use this book

The step-by-step chapters of this book include a few warm-up stretches followed by both core-stabilizing and core-strengthening exercises, as well as cool-downs. For each exercise, you'll find a short overview of the move, photos with step-by-step instructions demonstrating how to do it, some tips on how to perform it, and an anatomical illustration annotating key muscles. Some exercises have

Core and cardio

Core training isn't just about flat abs—a core-training regimen can also offer you a full-body workout that improves cardiovascular fitness.

Before you begin your exercise session, try a few High Knees to raise your heart rate. To perform this fat-burning move, begin running in place, raising your knees to waist height and staying on the balls of your feet. Be sure to keep your core engaged, and really pump your arms for extra aerobic benefit.

Exercises such as Mountain Climber (see pages 56–57) combine the best of core and cardio.

Working out at home

A clear plan and the will to improve are all you need to begin an at-home core-training regimen that is just as effective as working with a personal trainer at an exclusive gym.

You don't need a multilevel health club with all the latest equipment and extras in order to cultivate an attention-grabbing physique. In truth, some of the fittest bodies have been sculpted in low-tech gyms and even at home with some basic equipment—the only extras you'll need are the desire to improve and a targeted plan. In fact, a targeted fitness plan performed at home can prove superior to a schedule at a commercial health club that includes a daunting array of high-tech machinery and filled-up classes. At home, you can focus without distractions and work at your own pace, experimenting as you see fit in order to keep your exercise sessions interesting.

Home-gym equipment

Effective at-home core training calls for very few pieces of specialized equipment—your own body weight is your best asset, providing resistance. To add variety to your fitness regimen, take advantage of objects around the house: use a chair as a prop for dips and push-ups or take advantage of

steps for lunges. Broomsticks come in handy for balancing exercises and twisting movements. A large, thick towel or carpet will provide light cushioning and prevent you from sliding on the floor if you don't have a mat.

There are also plenty of relatively inexpensive pieces of equipment that change up your home workout. Hand weights or dumbbells add resistance, and they take up very little space. To keep clutter to a minimum, purchase adjustable dumbbells that allow you to easily vary the weight levels. Look for a set with a solid-locking mechanism that makes adding and subtracting weight disks a breeze.

You can also augment your workout with elastic resistance bands; anchoring one of these under your feet or attaching it

A core-training corner

Even in the smallest of homes, you can create a fully functional core-training area. Basically, your space need not be much larger than an exercise mat.

Lay out your mat away from the clutter of daily life, if possible. The fewer distractions you face, the more you can concentrate on your breathing, form, and speed. It's also convenient to have a closet or shelf nearby, so that you can store your fitness equipment, such as balls and weights, and set it up without fuss.

Devise a schedule for yourself, designating regular workout times to spend in your core-training corner. You want your training to become a habit.

Creating an inviting and invigorating corner will further your effort to make working out a habit. If simplicity appeals to you, keep your space spare and serene, but don't be afraid to bring in objects that inspire you. A large mirror or anatomical posters of the human skeleton and the major muscles of the back and front might make interesting additions to your space. Although not strictly necessary, these extra visuals can help keep you focused while also providing information that can enhance your exercise experience. The more the space appeals to you, the more you will want to go there.

Fitness balls

A low-tech extra like the antiburst fitness ball shown adds another dimension to your at-home routine. This heavy-duty inflatable ball—known by many names, including Swiss ball, exercise ball, body ball, and balance ball—was originally developed for use by physical therapy patients, but it is now standard equipment in commercial and home gyms everywhere. Working on a fitness ball, which ranges in diameter from 15 to 33 inches (35–85 cm), calls for you to constantly adjust your balance, which forces the engagement of many more muscles, especially those of your core. You can perform both core-stabilizing and core-strengthening exercises on a fitness ball.

to a sturdy object allows you to easily switch exercise angles and increase intensity. These bands, which come in several progressive resistance levels, add another layer of variety to your routine. Weighing next-to-nothing and taking up almost no space, they are the perfect pieces of equipment for travelers who want to keep up their fitness regimens even while away from home.

Balls have many uses in a core-training program. A weighted medicine ball can take the place of hand weights or dumbbells. A fitness ball, shown in many of the following exercises, is a large, heavy-duty inflatable ball that helps you improve your balance and flexibility.

Make sure that your workout surface is comfortable. If you are exercising on a mat, roll it out properly, making sure that it lies flat with no loose ends curling upward. Leave plenty of space around it. It is important that you be able to freely elongate your muscles; incomplete extensions can lead to incomplete muscular development. A full range of motion is vital to your progress.

Your workout wardrobe

Think comfort, utility, and, yes, style when deciding what to wear for your workout. Dress for breathability, insulation, and functional comfort, choosing garments that allow you to move freely. This doesn't mean that you should throw on a shapeless T-shirt or baggy sweatpants; form-fitting shorts and tops move with your natural musculature rather than restricting it. Even if you're working out at home, a great outfit can inspire you. Try exercising in front of a mirror—at the start of your workout plan, you may not like how you look in body-hugging garments, but as you stick to your plan, you'll see the changes to your shape even more clearly. Now that's motivation.

Invest in shoes with good cushioning and support; your feet are your foundation. You'll find core training–specific athletic shoes on the market, but a sturdy cross-trainer will serve your needs very well, too.

A time and place for fitness

Effective exercise begins with setting aside time and a place. This is your chance to give back to your body and maintain the machine that is you. Pick a distraction-free location that allows you to clearly focus on your fitness goals. Such elements as music, room temperature, and lighting all have effects on ensuring the best possible workout. A great thing about working out at home is that you can keep these elements personalized to your own taste.

Now that you are set to begin your workout, it is important that you be "present." This may seem like a no-brainer at first, but in today's ultra-fast-paced world, it is easy to become distracted by what you think you may be missing while working out. Try to leave all of your concerns outside of your workout space. Turn off the pads, pods, and various other electronic distractions—the world will still exist in all its complexity once your session is over.

For many, making time and space to take care of the body is the highest hurdle; simply getting ready to exercise, whether this involves driving to the gym or setting up a mat at home, takes discipline, time management, and commitment. But we all share the same 24 hours in a day; from the stay-at-home dad to the corporate executive, we lead busy lives. You absolutely can and must make the commitment to take care of your body, whether you slot in that 15 minutes before work, 20 minutes during lunchtime, or 30 minutes after dinner. Make the most of your 24 hours by bettering yourself.

Nourishing your core

Consistent exercise is only part of the successful core-training equation: you must combine targeted training with healthy nutrition to achieve a strong and healthy body.

When you train your core, you are aiming for a physique that is both low in visible body fat and high in lean muscle tissue—a physique most definitely attainable. You can maintain a fit core over the long term by carrying out a solid day-to-day plan that combines stretching, strengthening and cardiovascular exercise with sound food choices.

Food as fuel

For best results, it is vital to fuel properly. The old adage that you are what you eat applies quite literally to the physique. Almost anyone can get thin or even skinny—just severely limit food intake. Relying on drastic reductions of calories, though, often comes at the expense of precious muscle tissue. And a starvation diet usually results in a rebound effect, with the overzealous dieter soon gaining back all the lost weight and then some.

When it comes to fat loss, the most common mistake lies in overtraining and, in the process, breaking the body down to the point of lethargy and exhaustion, while also failing to eat enough to power the body. In this scenario, the body reacts to the lack of food as if it were facing true famine and will burn muscle tissue while holding on to fat stores it can reserve for future use. Your scale may display a lower number, but you still have the same amount of body fat as ever. Rid yourself of any fixation on low weight—replace a "skinny" mentality with a "lean" consciousness.

Too many of us skip breakfast or depend on a last-minute stimulant like coffee, which may fuel us through a few hours—but burnout is inevitable. For optimal results, consume small, frequent meals throughout the day in order to keep your body energized, sparing muscle and instead utilizing stored fat as fuel.

Balancing your diet

The food that makes up your diet can be divided into three groups, or macronutrients: proteins, which help to build muscle mass; fats, which are good for joint lubrication, maintaining body temperature, and promoting healthy cell function in your hair and skin; and carbohydrates, which provide energy.

Look not at calories but rather at macronutrients. Proteins, carbohydrates, and fats are the numbers with which successful "dieters" concern themselves. If you know how many grams of each you consume daily, your can calculate your total caloric intake by adding the three macronutrients.

Carbs: friend or foe?

Carbohydrates can be simple, complex, or fibrous. Simple carbs, such as fruit, are broken down quickly by the body and provide short bursts of energy, while complex carbs, such as oatmeal, are slower to break down and provide sustained energy for longer periods. Fibrous carbs like broccoli and asparagus aid digestion and provide fiber, which assists in the removal of waste from the body.

Many different theories surround the role of carbohydrates in the diet. To some they are the enemy, while others tout them as absolutely necessary parts of every meal. The truth is that they should have a place in the diet of anyone seeking to get fit and look great.

A rainbow diet

Eating the colors of the rainbow may sound like an elementary school lesson plan, but its underlying message is important for adults and children alike. Choose from a varied palette of fruits and vegetables from red berries to green spinach to violet plums—and all the shades in between. Splashing your plate with different-colored fruits and vegetables is an easy and smart way to ensure that you are getting the vitamins and minerals you need.

Eating to lose

A day of healthy eating doesn't mean 24 hours of depriving yourself. To lose fat and raise energy, think of your meals as regular refueling: consume 5 to 6 small meals every 3 hours or so. The key is to maintain a positive nitrogen balance and peak blood sugar levels, which you can accomplish by including some protein with every meal and ample carbs for optimal fueling throughout the day.

When planning your daily menu, include 3 whole meals, with 2 supplemental high-energy snacks, such as ready-to-drink protein shakes. The following is just a sample menu of a healthy day of eating.

Breakfast: An omelet made from two egg whites and one yolk, with a small bowl of oatmeal topped with strawberries

Morning snack: A protein shake and a handful of raw nuts

Lunch: Chicken-breast salad topped with kidney beans

Afternoon snack: A protein shake and a piece of fruit

Dinner: Baked fish, poached asparagus, and brown rice

If you are used to the typical deprivation-style weight-loss diet, you may at first feel as if you are eating too much, but you're really eating the same amount—just parceled into smaller packages. Your body will soon adjust to your new meal schedule; with the increased activity levels of your core training, it will come to expect to be fed every few hours or so. Remember: one must eat to lose.

All too often, when you want to lose weight, you begin your day with a carb-free breakfast, eat a midday meal like salad that is high in fibrous carbs, and then arrive home from work ravenous and proceed to consume an excess of complex and simple carbs. Starting out without carbs limits the energy you can draw upon throughout the day. A lunchtime salad, with lots of fibrous carbs but few if any complex ones, may leave you struggling to get through the next few hours. And consuming an overabundance of complex and simple carbs in the evening, when your body does not need this energy, is likely to result in stored fat. Following this eating pattern means that you are likely to wake up the next day noticeably softer—and liable to begin the process of carb restriction and then introduction all over again.

Instead, for optimal fueling and fat loss, eat breakfast like a king, lunch like a prince, and dinner like a pauper. Generally speaking, a ratio of 40 percent protein to 40 percent carbohydrates and 20 percent fats should compose your nutritional intake. Additionally, tapering your carb intake, starting with the largest portion early in the day before switching to more fibrous or low-caloric choices, will help to keep your fat furnace burning.

A recipe for fueling

Consume at least one gram of protein per pound of your body weight from lean sources (think lean beef, white-meat poultry, fish, eggs, low-fat cottage cheese, and Greek yogurt) in order to preserve and/or gain lean muscle mass. "Good" fats such as monounsaturated fats (found in olives and avocados, for instance), polyunsaturated fats (found in nuts and seeds), and omega-3s (found in walnuts, flax seeds, and coldwater oily fish such as salmon, sardines, and anchovies) will provide a feeling of satiety, help to lubricate your joints, moisturize your skin, and assist in protecting your heart.

Hydrate, hydrate

Consuming adequate fluid is another key factor in maximizing exercise performance and preventing injury. Proper hydration maintains optimal organ function and helps you feel your

exertion. Failure to replace fluids lost through perspiration, can produce serious effects. Early signs of dehydration include thirst, flushed skin, premature fatigue, accelerated pulse and breathing rates, and decreased exercise capacity. These symptoms can give way to dizziness and severe weakness if dehydration is allowed to persist. Most nutrition authorities recommend drinking water before, during, and after low- to moderate-intensity exercise that lasts up to an hour. Anyone exercising for more than an hour at a higher intensity should consume beverages that contain a combination of carbohydrates and electrolytes. A smart choice is 100-percent pure coconut water, which contains fewer calories and less sugar and sodium than many popular sports drinks. Another healthy way to replace fluids and electrolytes lost during exercise is to eat a serving of fruit or vegetables after your workout.

best during and after your core workout. It is healthy to work up a sweat while exercising; sweating is your body's way of protecting you from overheating during periods of physical

Trimming the fat

The healthy range for real, long-lasting fat loss is one to two pounds per week. You can best achieve this goal

The Glycemic Index

The Glycemic Index (GI), which some have found to be the nutritional key to long-term fat loss, measures the rate at which carbohydrates affect our blood sugar levels. A lower-GI food is likely to be digested at a relatively slow rate, impose a lower insulin demand on the body, and ultimately lead to less fat storage.

According to the Glycemic Index, foods with a high GI score of 70 and above include white bread, white rice, extruded breakfast cereals, and glucose. Those foods with a medium range of 56 to 69 include whole-wheat products, and sucrose (found in brown sugar and maple syrup, for instance). Foods considered to have a low GI score of 55 or below include most vegetables, legumes, whole grains, nuts, and fructose (found in colas and honey); for a lean physique, these low-GI foods should constitute the majority of carbohydrates consumed.

GI values of some common foods

Low GI 55 and below	Medium GI 56–69	High GI 70 and above
	(image)	
· apples	· angel food cake	· alcoholic drinks
· beets	· apricots	· bacon
· berries	· barley	· baked beans
· cherries	· brown rice	· broad beans
· chickpeas	· brown sugar	· butter
· citrus fruits	· cranberry juice	· corn flakes
· jams & marmalades	· croissants	· doughnuts
· kidney beans	· Danish pastries	· eggs
· lentils	· maple syrup	· French fries
· lettuce	· muesli	· ice cream
· milk (skim)	· muffins	· jelly beans
· nuts	· oat bran	· parsnips
· pasta	· pineapples	· potato chips
· peaches	· pita bread	· pretzels
· peppers	· pizza	· puffed wheat
· plums	· popcorn	· sausages
· snow peas	· pumpernickel bread	· waffles
· spinach	· raisins	· watermelons
· tomatoes	· rye bread	· white bread
· wheat kernels	· shortbread	· white potatoes
· yogurt (low-fat)	· shredded wheat	· white rice

Vitamins and supplements

It is always best to obtain nutrients from whole foods. If you find certain nutrient-rich foods unpalatable or they aren't readily available where you live, however, then it is crucial to take a multivitamin that contains at least 100 percent of the recommended daily value (DV) for the nutrients you need. This information can be found on the supplement package.

through a combination of good nutrition (to fuel the body), proper weight training (to harden the body), and ample cardiovascular activity (to burn stored fat). When these three elements are all strong, your body will support you time and time again—and you'll see real improvement, as well.

Sticking to the plan

If you're like so many of us these days, trying to fit as much as possible into a hectic schedule, you often skip meals and snack on highly processed sugar-laden foods during lunchtime, only to come home later at night and gorge on anything and everything in sight. The result is a constant yo-yo game of weight gain and weight loss.

A better plan: follow a "grazing" system of several small meals consumed throughout the day. This system keeps energy levels up and encourages the body to use fat as its fuel source.

Of course, life isn't a never-ending sprint toward optimum condition, but rather a steady jog to a healthy and consistent

baseline. Every once in a while you may peak for an athletic event (a race or marathon, for instance) or a special occasion (like a wedding or reunion), but aim for healthy eating and effective exercise as a consistent lifestyle. You'll look great, and will function well, too.

A healthy lifestyle means enjoying your life, so even as you begin your any diet, factor in the occasional indulgence or "cheat" meal. Rather than sabotaging your efforts, a treat can offset the mental fatigue that often accompanies strenuous dieting. Have your cheat meal when needed (once or twice per week), and then return to your diet.

Eating out and eating healthy

All you need is a bit of planning to make sure that you eat healthy whether dining at home, at work, or at a restaurant. With a little effort the night before, you can prepare a nutritious lunch for the next workday. Grilling some chicken breast or microwaving some yams and vegetables yields a balanced lunch. A small bag of raw nuts and a couple of pieces of fruit makes the perfect midafternoon snack. The fewer processed foods (breads, cereals, sauces) you consume, the more efficiently your body will run.

Feel free to join your friends for an evening out sharing a meal—just choose the most healthful menu options. At a Chinese restaurant, order steamed chicken, vegetables, and brown rice with sauce on the side. At a Mexican restaurant indulge in the grilled chicken or shrimp over a salad and black beans topped with salsa. At an Italian restaurant, look for grilled chicken or fish over whole-wheat pasta and a light tomato sauce; at a Mediterranean restaurant, opt for the hummus over a salad with a whole-wheat pita. No matter what the cuisine, you always have a healthy choice.

Full-body anatomy

Front View

Annotation Key
* indicates deep muscles

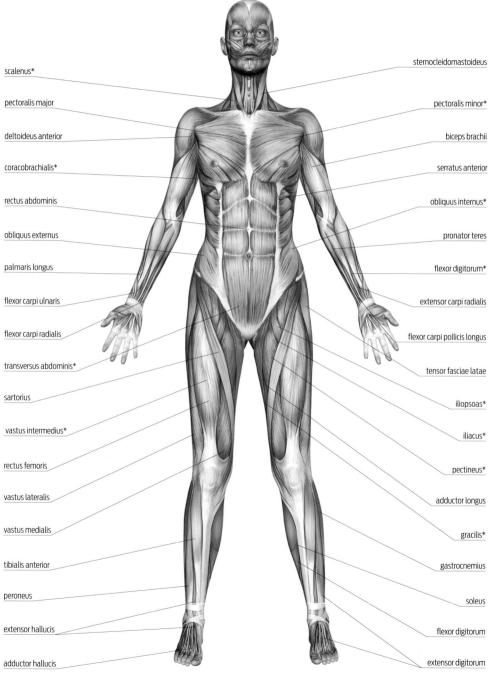

scalenus*

pectoralis major

deltoideus anterior

coracobrachialis*

rectus abdominis

obliquus externus

palmaris longus

flexor carpi ulnaris

flexor carpi radialis

transversus abdominis*

sartorius

vastus intermedius*

rectus femoris

vastus lateralis

vastus medialis

tibialis anterior

peroneus

extensor hallucis

adductor hallucis

sternocleidomastoideus

pectoralis minor*

biceps brachii

serratus anterior

obliquus internus*

pronator teres

flexor digitorum*

extensor carpi radialis

flexor carpi pollicis longus

tensor fasciae latae

iliopsoas*

iliacus*

pectineus*

adductor longus

gracilis*

gastrocnemius

soleus

flexor digitorum

extensor digitorum

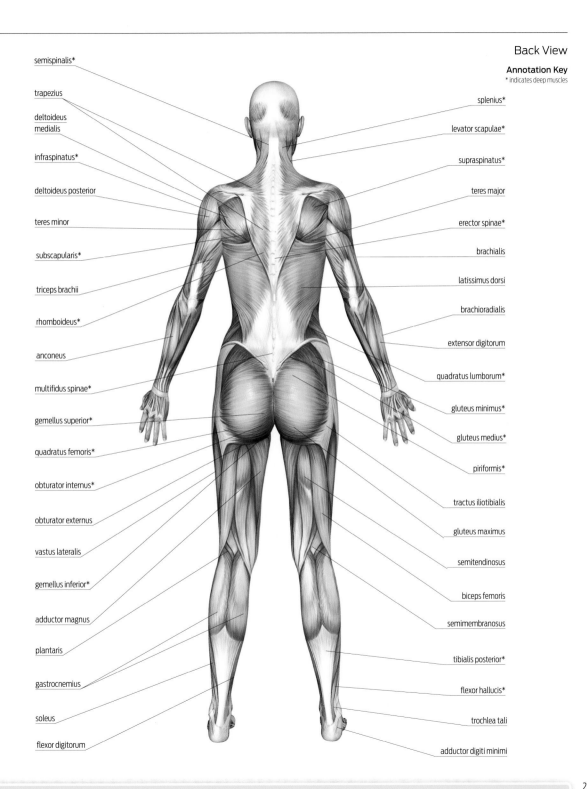

Back View

Annotation Key
* indicates deep muscles

semispinalis*

trapezius

deltoideus
medialis

infraspinatus*

deltoideus posterior

teres minor

subscapularis*

triceps brachii

rhomboideus*

anconeus

multifidus spinae*

gemellus superior*

quadratus femoris*

obturator internus*

obturator externus

vastus lateralis

gemellus inferior*

adductor magnus

plantaris

gastrocnemius

soleus

flexor digitorum

splenius*

levator scapulae*

supraspinatus*

teres major

erector spinae*

brachialis

latissimus dorsi

brachioradialis

extensor digitorum

quadratus lumborum*

gluteus minimus*

gluteus medius*

piriformis*

tractus iliotibialis

gluteus maximus

semitendinosus

biceps femoris

semimembranosus

tibialis posterior*

flexor hallucis*

trochlea tali

adductor digiti minimi

Contents

Supine Lower-Back Stretch 24

Side Stretch 25

Half-Kneeling Rotation........26

Are you ready to really work your core, pushing yourself to the limit? The following sample of warm-up exercises will prepare your muscles for the core-training regimen to come. Warming up properly reduces your risk of injury, so make warming up a ritual that you complete at the start of every core-training workout, and include a few cardio exercises, such as running in place or jumping jacks, that get your heart pumping and your spirit energized. Your core muscles will thank you.

Warm-Ups

Level
· Beginner

Duration
· 2–3 minutes

Benefits
· Stretches lower-back and gluteal muscles

Caution
· Severe back issues

Back & Side Stretches

Supine Lower-Back Stretch

Supine Lower-Back Stretch is an excellent warm-up that stretches your lower-back and gluteal muscles, preparing them for the workout ahead.

1 Lie on your back, with legs bent and hands clasped around your knees.

2 Slowly pull your knees toward your chest until you feel a stretch in your lower back.

3 Hold for 30 seconds, relax, and repeat for an additional 30 seconds.

Annotation Key
Bold text indicates target muscles
Black text indicates other working muscles
* indicates deep muscles

Back View

quadratus lumborum*

piriformis*
gluteus maximus

biceps femoris

semitendinosus

latissimus dorsi

erector spinae*

gluteus medius*

semimembranosus

Correct form
· Keep your knees and feet together.

Avoid
· Raising your head off the floor.

Side Stretch

When performing Side Stretch, you should feel a good stretch along the sides of your body. Focus on keeping the lower part of your body strongly rooted and stable, like a tree with branches leaning over in the wind.

1 Stand with one hand on your hip and the other arm over your head and leaning toward the opposite side.

2 Reach up and over, and lean your torso to the side.

3 Hold for 30 seconds, relax, and repeat for an additional 30 seconds.

Level
· Beginner

Duration
· 2–3 minutes

Benefits
· Stretches upper back and core

Caution
· Severe back issues

Annotation Key
Bold text indicates target muscles
Black text indicates other working muscles
* indicates deep muscles

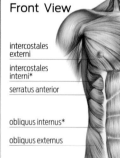

Front View

intercostales externi

intercostales interni*

serratus anterior

obliquus internus*

obliquus externus

Back View

trapezius

deltoideus posterior

teres minor

teres major

latissimus dorsi

erector spinae*

multifidus spinae*

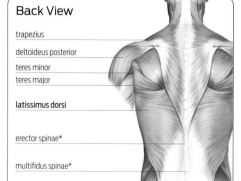

Correct form
· Be sure to keep your torso straight on.

Avoid
· Bending forward or backward at the trunk.

Half-Kneeling Rotation

Half-Kneeling Rotation is a warm-up stretch that increases your spinal mobility, improves your posture, and enhances your core rotation. Concentrate on engaging your core muscles, making sure that your stomach does not bulge outward as your upper body rotates from one side to the other.

1 Kneel on one leg with your right leg bent at 90 degrees in front of you, foot on the floor. Your hands should be beside your head and your elbows should be flared outward.

2 Keeping your back straight, rotate your left shoulder toward your right knee.

3 Hold for 10 seconds, and then repeat on the other side. Work up to 10 repetitions on each side.

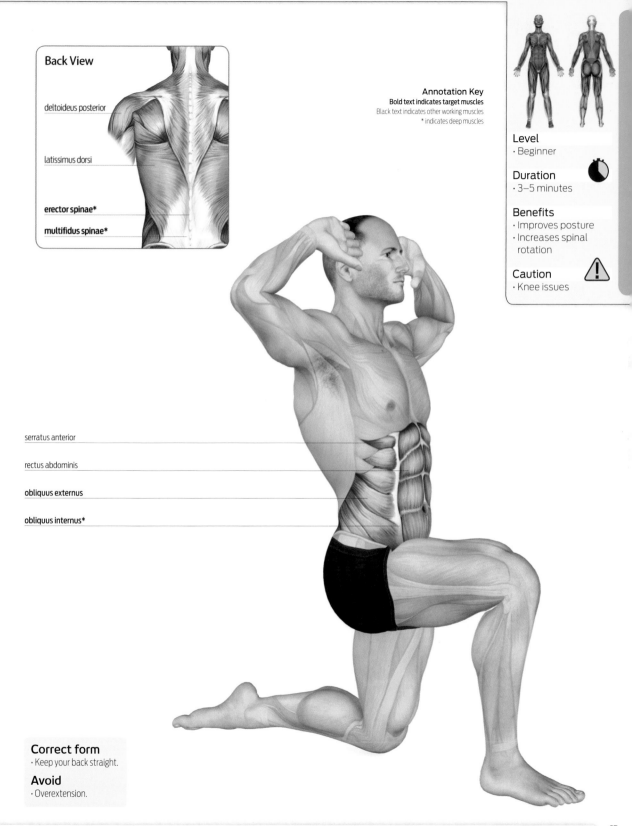

Back View

deltoideus posterior

latissimus dorsi

erector spinae*

multifidus spinae*

Annotation Key
Bold text indicates target muscles
Black text indicates other working muscles
* indicates deep muscles

Level
· Beginner

Duration
· 3–5 minutes

Benefits
· Improves posture
· Increases spinal rotation

Caution
· Knee issues

serratus anterior

rectus abdominis

obliquus externus

obliquus internus*

Correct form
· Keep your back straight.

Avoid
· Overextension.

Contents

Plank.........................30

Plank-Up.....................32

Side Plank...................34

Side Plank with
Reach-Under.................36

Side Plank with Band Row 38

Fire-Hydrant In-Out 40

T-Stabilization 42

Fitness Ball Atomic Push-Up .. 44

Fitness Ball Pike.............. 46

Fitness Ball Jackknife 48

Fitness Ball Lateral Roll 50

Fitness Ball Rollout 52

Fitness Ball Hyperextension....54

Mountain Climber 56

Body-Weight Squat 58

Medicine Ball Squat to Press .. 60

Balance Push-Up..............62

Kneel on Ball 64

Medicine Ball
Over-the-Shoulder Throw 66

Fitness Ball Split Squat 68

Fitness Ball Prone
Row to External Rotation 70

Fitness Ball Seated
External Rotation 72

Medicine Ball Walkover.........74

Fitness Ball Band Fly 76

Fitness Ball Walk-Around 78

Medicine Ball
Pullover on Fitness Ball 80

Side Lunge and Press..........82

Hip Crossover 84

Hip Raise 86

Fitness Ball Hip Raise......... 88

Fitness Ball Bridge 90

Stiff-Legged Deadlift..........92

Standing One-Legged Row.... 94

Your abdominals, obliques, glutes, hip adductors, hip flexors, and spinal column work together to support you each and every day. It's only right, then, that you should put some effort into supporting them.

The following exercises make for a more stable core, which will augment your performance as you move through a spectrum of daily activities. Whether you are reaching for the high shelf at the supermarket, running for the bus, or swinging a baseball bat, performing these exercises will build a more balanced, centered, and powerful body. So try holding that Side Plank 10 seconds longer than usual, or making T-Stabilization a morning ritual.

Core Stabilizers

Plank

Plank is an isometric, or contracted, core-stabilizing exercise, designed to work your entire core. It is performed everywhere from yoga and Pilates studios to hard-core gyms for a good reason: it is a reliable way to build endurance in your abs and back, as well as in the stabilizer muscles.

1 Kneel on an exercise mat, and then place your hands on the floor to come into onto all-fours.

2 Plant your forearms on the floor, parallel to each other.

Correct form
· Keep your abdominal muscles tight.
· Keep your body in a straight line.

Avoid
· Bridging too high, which can take stress off working muscles.

3 Raise your knees off the floor and lengthen your legs until they are in line with your arms. Remain suspended in Plank for 30 seconds, building up to 2 minutes.

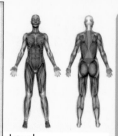

Front View

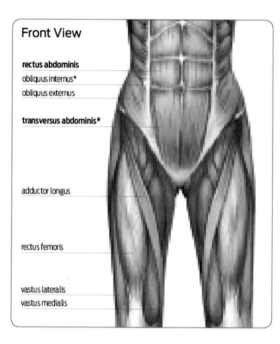

rectus abdominis
obliquus internus*
obliquus externus

transversus abdominis*

adductor longus

rectus femoris

vastus lateralis
vastus medialis

Annotation Key
Bold text indicates target muscles
Black text indicates other working muscles
* indicates deep muscles

Level
· Beginner

Duration
· 30 seconds–
2 minutes

Benefits
· Stabilizes trunk
and pelvis
· Builds strength

Caution
· Shoulder issues
· Lower-back issues

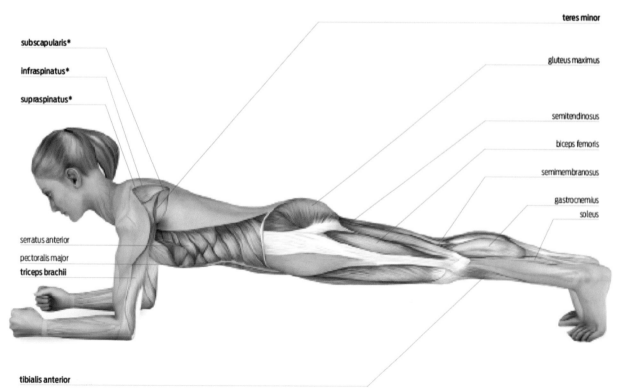

subscapularis*

infraspinatus*

supraspinatus*

serratus anterior
pectoralis major
triceps brachii

tibialis anterior

teres minor

gluteus maximus

semitendinosus

biceps femoris

semimembranosus

gastrocnemius
soleus

Plank-Up

Plank-Up is an advanced core-stabilizing
exercise that expands upon the basic Plank
exercise. Try to maintain a steady rhythm
as you move from one arm to the other.

1 Begin on your hands and knees in
a facedown position. Plant your
forearms on the floor parallel to each other.

2 Raise your knees off the floor and
lengthen your legs until they are in line
with your arms.

3 Lift up with your right arm until it is fully
extended, and then straighten your left
arm until you are balanced on both arms in a
completed push-up position.

Correct form
· Plant each hand, rather than using
  momentum, which places too
  much stress on the joints.
· Keep your abs tucked tightly during
  the movement.

Avoid
· Crashing down suddenly; instead,
  use a steady 4-count motion: 2 up
  for both arms, then 2 down.

4 Reverse one arm at a time, lowering from the planted hand to forearm until back in the initial plank position. Begin with 10 complete repetitions and work up to 2 sets of 15.

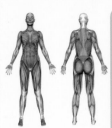

Level
· Advanced

Duration
· 2–3 minutes

Benefits
· Stabilizes trunk and pelvis
· Builds strength

Caution
· Pregnancy
· Rotator cuff injury

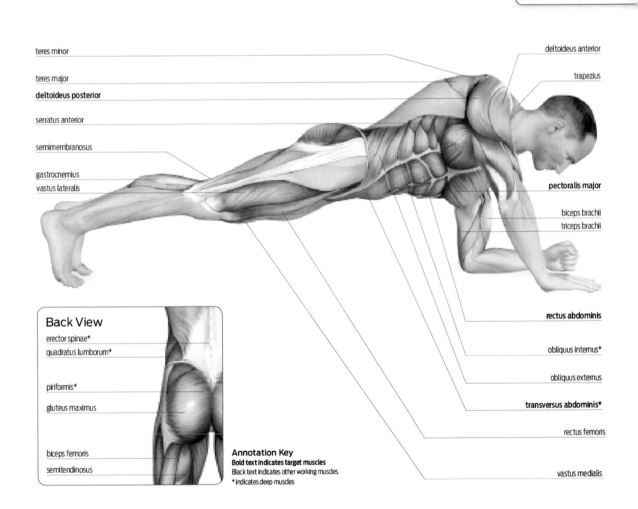

teres minor

teres major

deltoideus posterior

serratus anterior

semimembranosus

gastrocnemius
vastus lateralis

deltoideus anterior

trapezius

pectoralis major

biceps brachii
triceps brachii

rectus abdominis

obliquus internus*

obliquus externus

transversus abdominis*

rectus femoris

vastus medialis

Back View
erector spinae*
quadratus lumborum*

piriformis*

gluteus maximus

biceps femoris

semitendinosus

Annotation Key
Bold text indicates target muscles
Black text indicates other working muscles
* indicates deep muscles

Side Plank

Side Plank stabilizes your spine, but it is also great for strengthening your abdominals, lower back, and shoulders. Contracting your abdominals in Side Plank is a great way to whittle down your waistline. For best results, try holding for a few seconds longer than you initially think you can.

Correct form
· Push evenly from both your forearm and hips.

Avoid
· Placing too much strain on your shoulders; they should neither sink into their sockets nor lift toward your ears.

1 Lie on your left side with your legs straight and parallel to each other. Keep your feet flexed.

2 Bend your left arm to form a 90-degree angle with the knuckles of your hand facing forward. Place your right hand on your waist or extend your arm along your side.

3 Pressing your forearm down into the floor, raise your hips until your body is in a long, straight line. Hold for 30 seconds, working up to 1 minute. Release, and repeat on the other side.

Back View

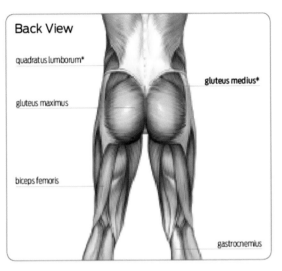

quadratus lumborum*

gluteus medius*

gluteus maximus

biceps femoris

gastrocnemius

Annotation Key
Bold text indicates target muscles
Black text indicates other working muscles
* indicates deep muscles

Level
· Advanced

Duration
· 4 minutes

Benefits
· Stabilizes trunk
  and spine
· Strengthens glutes,
  back, and abs

Caution
· Neck issues
· Rotator cuff injury

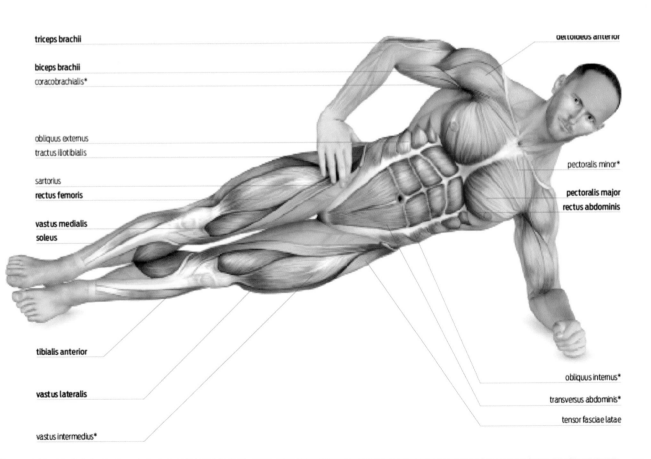

triceps brachii

biceps brachii
coracobrachialis*

obliquus externus
tractus iliotibialis

sartorius
rectus femoris

vastus medialis
soleus

tibialis anterior

vastus lateralis

vastus intermedius*

deltoideus anterior

pectoralis minor*

pectoralis major
rectus abdominis

obliquus internus*

transversus abdominis*

tensor fasciae latae

Side Plank with Reach-Under

In Side Plank with Reach-Under, strength lies in stillness rather than in motion. As you maintain the static position of your torso and legs while moving one of your arms, you are effectively strengthening your abs, lower back, and shoulders.

1 Lie on your left side with your legs straight and parallel to each other. Keep your feet flexed.

2 Bend your left arm to form a 90-degree angle, with the knuckles of your hand facing forward. Place your right hand on your waist or extend your arm along your side.

3 Pressing your left forearm into the floor, raise your hips off the floor until your body forms a long, straight line.

4 Twist your upper torso toward the floor as you reach your right arm under your chest as far as you can stretch.

5 Twist your upper torso back to front as you extend your right arm toward the ceiling.

6 Complete 4 repetitions, and then switch sides and repeat. Work up to performing 2 sets of 15 on each side.

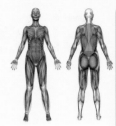

Correct form
· Both your forearm and your hips should drive the raising motion.
· Allow your head and neck to follow the movement of your torso, so that you are looking toward the floor during the reach-under and straight ahead in the finished position with your top arm extended.
· Keep your feet flexed and stacked.

Avoid
· Placing too much strain on your shoulders.
· Losing your alignment when your top arm is extended.

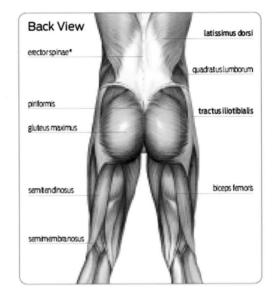

Back View

erector spinae*

piriformis

gluteus maximus

semitendinosus

semimembranosus

latissimus dorsi

quadratus lumborum

tractus iliotibialis

biceps femoris

Level
· Advanced

Duration
· 2–6 minutes

Benefits
· Strengthens and stabilizes core
· Builds endurance
· Strengthens shoulders

Caution
· Neck issues
· Rotator cuff injury

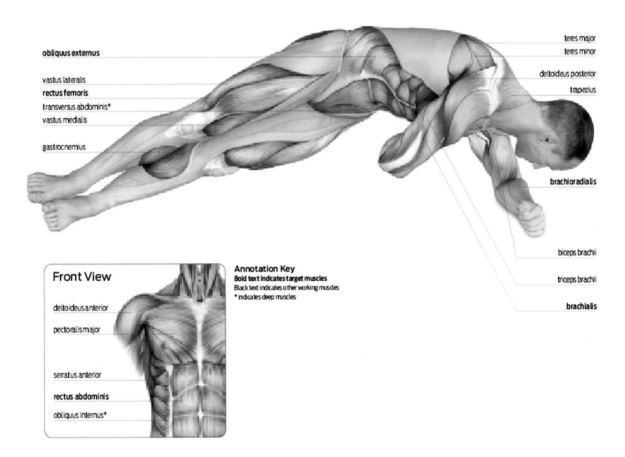

obliquus externus

vastus lateralis
rectus femoris
transversus abdominis*
vastus medialis

gastrocnemius

teres major
teres minor

deltoideus posterior

trapezius

brachioradialis

biceps brachii

triceps brachii

brachialis

Front View

deltoideus anterior

pectoralis major

serratus anterior

rectus abdominis

obliquus internus*

Annotation Key
Bold text indicates target muscles
Black text indicates other working muscles
* indicates deep muscles

Side Plank with Band Row

Side Plank with Band Row is an effective strengthener for your abdominal muscles, as well as the muscles in your upper and lower back and shoulders. As you pull the band and then release it, concentrate on moving your top arm smoothly and with control as the rest of your body stays still.

1 Attach one end of the exercise band to a nearby stabilized object. Lie on your left side, with your legs straight, stacked one on top of the other.

2 Bend your left arm so that if forms a 90-degree angle, with the knuckles of your hand facing forward.

Correct form
- Both your forearm and your hips should drive the raising motion.
- Make sure the band is pulled taut in the contracted position.
- Keep your legs stable throughout the exercise.
- Pull the band all the way to your chest.

Avoid
- Tensing either of your shoulders.
- Losing alignment in your body.

3 With your right arm, grasp one end of the exercise band. Extend your top arm in front of you, holding the band parallel to the floor.

4 Push off your forearm while raising your hips off the floor until your body forms one straight line.

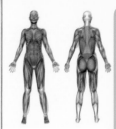

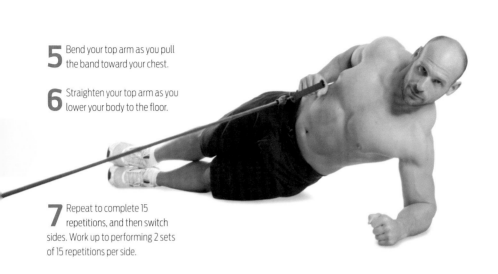

5 Bend your top arm as you pull the band toward your chest.

6 Straighten your top arm as you lower your body to the floor.

7 Repeat to complete 15 repetitions, and then switch sides. Work up to performing 2 sets of 15 repetitions per side.

Level
· Advanced

Duration
· 3 minutes

Benefits
· Strengthens and stabilizes core
· Strengthens arms

Caution
· Neck issues
· Rotator cuff injury

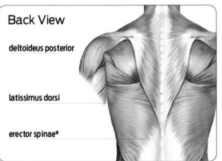

Back View

deltoideus posterior

latissimus dorsi

erector spinae*

Annotation Key
Bold text indicates target muscles
Black text indicates other working muscles
* indicates deep muscles

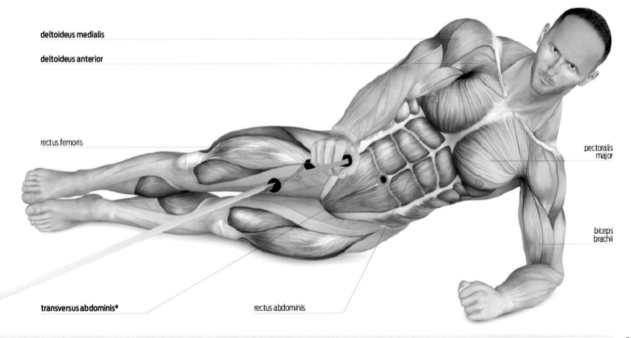

deltoideus medialis

deltoideus anterior

rectus femoris

pectoralis major

biceps brachii

transversus abdominis*

rectus abdominis

Fire-Hydrant In-Out

Fire Hydrant In-Out is a hard-working core-stabilizing exercise, as well as a great abdominal strengthener. It targets your inner thighs, hamstrings, and glutes, with assistance from your abdominal muscles.

Correct form
· Press your hands into the floor to keep your shoulders from sinking.
· Squeeze your glutes with your leg fully extended.

Avoid
· Lifting your hip as you lift your bent leg to the side.
· Rushing through the exercise; make sure that you feel each portion of the repetition.

1 Begin on your hands and knees, with your palms on the floor and spaced shoulder-width apart. Your spine should be in a neutral position.

2 Keeping your right leg bent at a 90-degree angle, raise it laterally, or to the side.

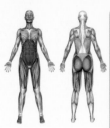

3 Straighten your right leg until it is fully extended behind you so that it is in line with your torso.

4 Bend your right knee and bring your leg back into its 90-degree position, and then lower it to meet your left leg. Work up to 15 repetitions. Repeat on the other side.

Level
· Beginner

Duration
· 3 minutes

Benefits
· Stabilizes pelvis
· Strengthens glutes

Caution

· Wrist pain
· Knee issues

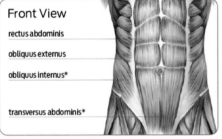

Front View
rectus abdominis

obliquus externus

obliquus internus*

transversus abdominis*

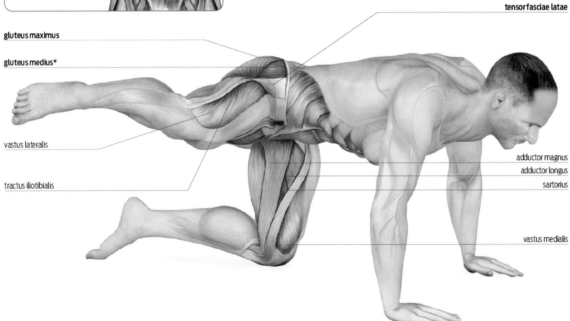

tensor fasciae latae

gluteus maximus

gluteus medius*

vastus lateralis

tractus iliotibialis

adductor magnus

adductor longus

sartorius

vastus medialis

T-Stabilization

T-Stabilization, another advanced variation on the traditional Plank, is a proven exercise for targeting your abs, hips, lower back, and obliques.

1 Assume the finished push-up position with your arms extended to full lockout, your fingers facing forward, your legs outstretched, and your body weight supported on your toes.

2 Turn your hips to one side, stacking one foot on top of the other and raising your top arm across your body until you are pointing toward the ceiling.

3 Hold for 30 seconds, lower, and then repeat on the other side. Work your way up to holding for 1 minute on each side.

Correct form
· Keep your body in one straight line.

Avoid
· Arching or bridging your back.

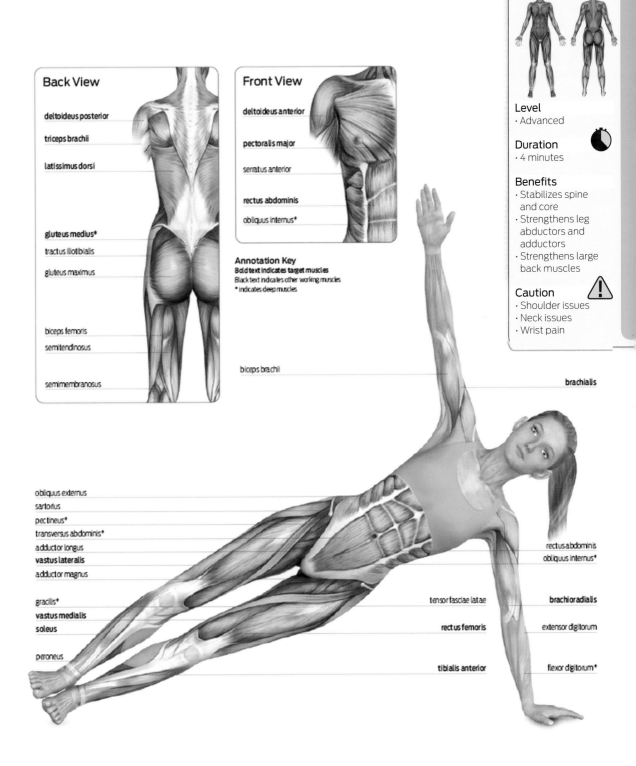

Back View

deltoideus posterior

triceps brachii

latissimus dorsi

gluteus medius*

tractus iliotibialis

gluteus maximus

biceps femoris

semitendinosus

semimembranosus

Front View

deltoideus anterior

pectoralis major

serratus anterior

rectus abdominis

obliquus internus*

Annotation Key
Bold text indicates target muscles
Black text indicates other working muscles
* indicates deep muscles

Level
· Advanced

Duration
· 4 minutes

Benefits
· Stabilizes spine
  and core
· Strengthens leg
  abductors and
  adductors
· Strengthens large
  back muscles

Caution
· Shoulder issues
· Neck issues
· Wrist pain

biceps brachii

brachialis

obliquus externus
sartorius
pectineus*
transversus abdominis*
adductor longus
vastus lateralis
adductor magnus

gracilis*
vastus medialis
soleus

peroneus

tensor fasciae latae

rectus femoris

tibialis anterior

rectus abdominis
obliquus internus*

brachioradialis

extensor digitorum

flexor digitorum*

Fitness Ball Atomic Push-Up

Performing the Fitness Ball Atomic Push-Up causes many major muscle groups to fire at once. When executed properly, this exercise tones your upper body, engages your core, and works your hip flexors.

1 Begin on your hands and knees with your fingers facing forward and a fitness ball placed behind you. Rest your shins on the ball, and straighten your legs so that your body forms a straight line.

2 While keeping your back flat, bend your knees to draw the fitness ball into your core.

Correct form
· Keep your hips level with your torso.

Avoid
· Piking or bridging your body.

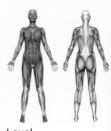

3 Straighten your legs, moving the ball farther behind you, and then perform a push-up. Start with 5 repetitions, working your way up to 2 sets of 12 to 15.

Level
· Advanced

Duration
· 2 minutes

Benefits
· Stabilizes spine and core

Caution
· Lower-back pain
· Wrist pain
· Shoulder issues

Front View

tensor fasciae latae

iliopsoas*
pectineus*

sartorius
adductor brevis
adductor longus

gracilis*

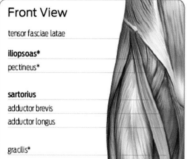

Annotation Key
Bold text indicates target muscles
Black text indicates other working muscles
* indicates deep muscles

obliquus externus

transversus abdominis*

obliquus internus*

rectus abdominis

deltoideus posterior

deltoideus anterior

brachialis
biceps brachii

triceps brachii
rectus femoris

tibialis anterior
vastus lateralis

Fitness Ball Pike

Fitness Ball Pike targets your hip flexors and external obliques, as well as your rectus abdominis and spinal erectors. In starting position, your sense of balance comes into play, and as you raise your hips your core muscles are greatly challenged. For best results, concentrate on keeping your movement smooth.

Correct form
· Raise your hips evenly.
· Move as slowly as possible.
· Keep both hands anchored to the floor.
· Keep your gaze directed toward the floor.

Avoid
· Rounding your back.
· Tilting your hips to either side.
· Straining your neck by trying to look forward.

1 Assume a push-up position with your arms shoulder-width apart and your shins resting on a fitness ball.

2 While keeping your legs straight, roll the ball toward your body while raising your hips as high as you are able.

3 Lower and repeat, performing 20 repetitions. Rest if desired, and then complete another set of 20.

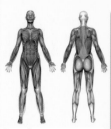

Level
· Advanced

Duration
· 2 minutes

Benefits
· Stabilizes core
· Strengthens abs
· Strengthens
  hip flexors

Caution
· Lower-back issues
· Shoulder issues
· Neck issues

Front View

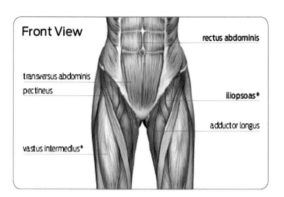

rectus abdominis

transversus abdominis

pectineus

iliopsoas*

adductor longus

vastus intermedius*

Back View

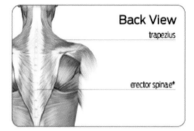

trapezius

erector spinae*

Annotation Key
Bold text indicates target muscles
Black text indicates other working muscles
* indicates deep muscles

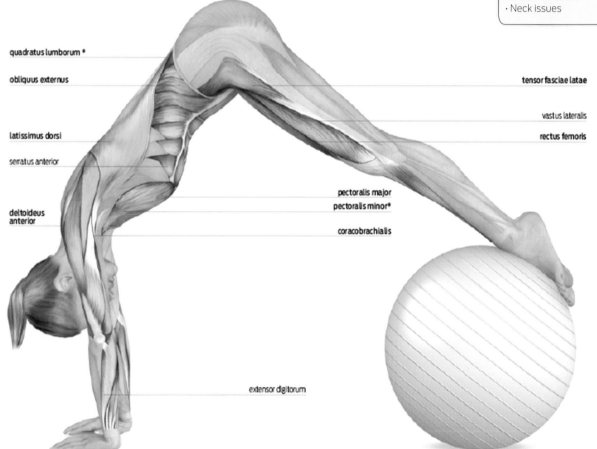

quadratus lumborum *

obliquus externus

latissimus dorsi

serratus anterior

deltoideus
anterior

tensor fasciae latae

vastus lateralis

rectus femoris

pectoralis major
pectoralis minor*

coracobrachialis

extensor digitorum

Fitness Ball Jackknife

Fitness Ball Jackknifes does an excellent job of working your hip flexors. It also targets both the front and back core muscles—especially your rectus abdominis and spinal erectors respectively.

Correct form
· Brace your core.
· Keep both hands anchored to the floor.
· Keep your gaze directed toward the floor.

Avoid
· Rounding your back.
· Straining your neck by trying to look forward.

1 Assume a push-up position with your arms shoulder-width apart and your shins resting on a fitness ball.

2 Bend your knees and roll the ball in towards your chest.

3 Slowly extend your legs, rolling the ball back to starting position.

4 Perform 20 repetitions. Rest if desired, and then complete another set of 20.

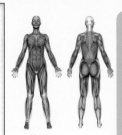

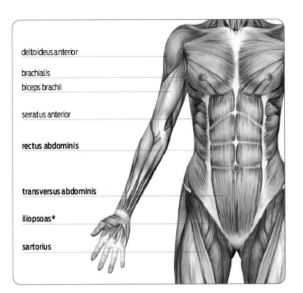

deltoideus anterior

brachialis

biceps brachii

serratus anterior

rectus abdominis

transversus abdominis

iliopsoas*

sartorius

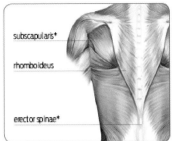

subscapularis*

rhomboideus

erector spinae*

Annotation Key
Bold text indicates target muscles
Black text indicates other working muscles
* indicates deep muscles

Level
· Advanced

Duration
· 2 minutes

Benefits
· Stabilizes core
· Strengthens abs
· Strengthens
  hip flexors

Caution
· Lower-back issues
· Shoulder issues
· Neck issues

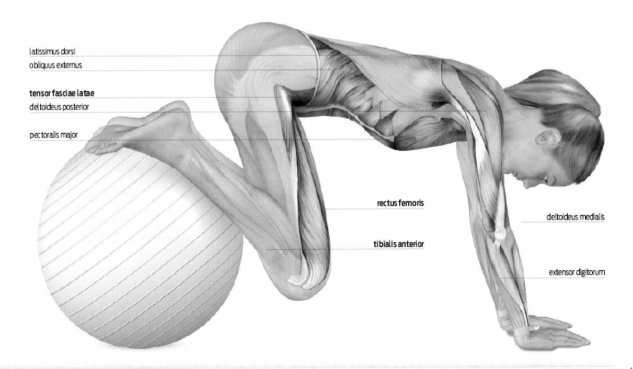

latissimus dorsi

obliquus externus

tensor fasciae latae

deltoideus posterior

pectoralis major

rectus femoris

tibialis anterior

deltoideus medialis

extensor digitorum

Fitness Ball Lateral Roll

Fitness Ball Lateral Roll offers a unique, dynamic way to build core stability. It calls for you to fully engage your core and rely on your balance and stability to drive the subtle movement.

1 Lie face-up on a fitness ball, with your upper back firmly supported. Plant your feet shoulder-width apart or a little wider. Your hips and thighs should be parallel to your torso; if necessary, raise your hips to achieve this alignment.

2 Extend your arms out to the sides.

3 Take "baby steps" as you move toward the side of the ball.

4 Take equally small steps back to the center of the ball.

5 Repeat on the other side. Complete 3 sets of 10 per side.

Annotation Key
Bold text indicates target muscles
Black text indicates other working muscles
* indicates deep muscles

Level
· Intermediate

Duration
· 4 minutes

Benefits
· Stabilizes core
· Strengthens abs
  and quadriceps

Caution
· Lower-back issues
· Neck issues

triceps brachii

rectus abdominis
iliopsoas*
adductor longus
adductor magnus
vastus intermedius*

obliquus internus*
transversus abdominis
obliquus externus
sartorius

adductor brevis

tensor fasciae latae

rectus femoris

vastus medialis

Correct form
· Keep your core braced.
· Keep your hips raised.
· Keep both arms extended.

Avoid
· Dropping your hips.
· Moving to the side too quickly.

Fitness Ball Rollout

Fitness Ball Rollout is a fun and challenging exercise
for effectively stabilizing your core. Aim for controlled,
steady movement throughout.

1 Kneel behind a fitness ball, with your fists
resting on top of it.

2 Extend the ball forward, leading with your
arms and following with your body until you
are completely stretched out while maintaining a
flat back and staying anchored on your knees.

3 Using your abdominals and lower back, roll
back in until you reach an upright position.

4 Repeat, working up to 3 sets of 15.

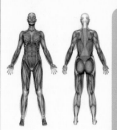

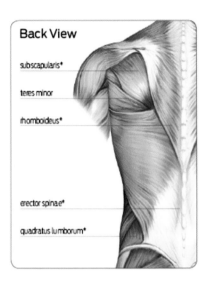

Back View

subscapularis*

teres minor

rhomboideus*

erector spinae*

quadratus lumborum*

Correct form
· Keep your body elongated.

Avoid
· Bridging your back and
  allowing your hips to sag.

Level
· Intermediate

Duration
· 3 minutes

Benefits
· Builds strength
  and dexterity

Caution
· Pregnancy
· Lower-back issues

Annotation Key
Bold text indicates target muscles
Black text indicates other working muscles
* indicates deep muscles

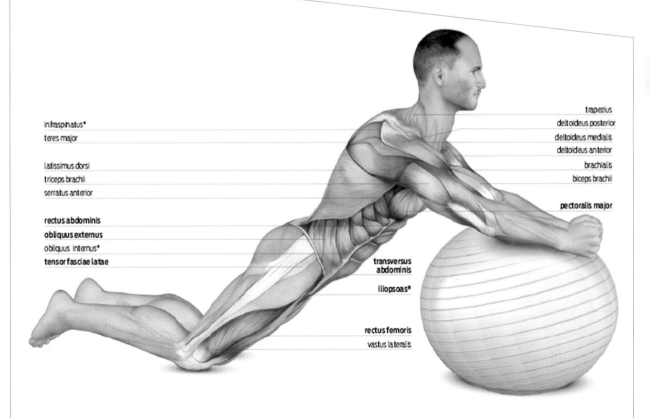

infraspinatus*

teres major

latissimus dorsi

triceps brachii

serratus anterior

rectus abdominis

obliquus externus

obliquus internus*

tensor fasciae latae

transversus
abdominis

iliopsoas*

rectus femoris

vastus lateralis

trapezius

deltoideus posterior

deltoideus medialis

deltoideus anterior

brachialis

biceps brachii

pectoralis major

Fitness Ball Hyperextension

Fitness Ball Hyperextension, executed on the large fitness ball, is a safe and effective alternative to traditional hyperextension machines. Performing this exercise is a great way to work your lower-back muscles.

1 Begin in a facedown position on top of a fitness ball, with your abdominals covering most of the ball, your legs spread with toes on the floor, and your arms behind your head. Push your toes into the floor for stability.

2 Raise your torso so that it forms a line with the lower half of your body.

3 Squeeze your glutes as you lower your upper body, and then raise it back to the starting position.

4 Continue lowering and raising, working up to 3 sets of 15 to 20.

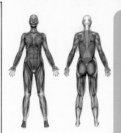

Front View

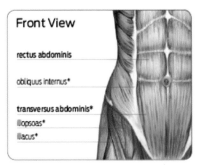

rectus abdominis

obliquus internus*

transversus abdominis*
iliopsoas*
iliacus*

Back View

trapezius
deltoideus medialis
deltoideus posterior
infraspinatus*
subscapularis*

rhomboideus*

erector spinae *

Correct form
· Complete the full range of motion in both the negative (downward stretch) and positive (upward motion) of the exercise.

Avoid
· Overcontracting or hyperextending your back at the top of the movement.

Level
· Intermediate

Duration
· 5 minutes

Benefits
· Strengthens gluteal and lower-back muscles

Caution ⚠
· Lower-back issues
· Neck issues

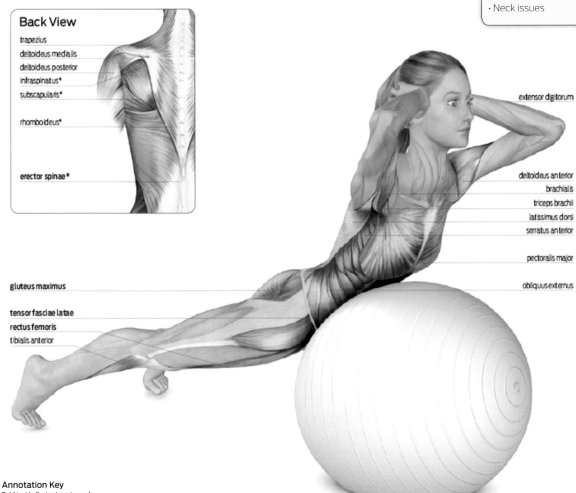

extensor digitorum

deltoideus anterior
brachialis
triceps brachii
latissimus dorsi
serratus anterior

pectoralis major

obliquus externus

gluteus maximus

tensor fasciae latae
rectus femoris
tibialis anterior

Annotation Key
Bold text indicates target muscles
Black text indicates other working muscles
* indicates deep muscles

Mountain Climber

Mountain Climber is a core-stabilizing, timed distance exercise. This high-intensity move gets your heart rate going, improving your cardiovascular fitness, while it challenges your legs and core. This all-around exercise also helps to develop muscular endurance in your arms.

1 Begin in a completed push-up position with your body forming a straight line.

2 Bend one knee, and bring it as close to your chest as possible.

3 Return to the starting position and repeat with your other leg. Continue to alternate for 30 seconds, working up to 2 minutes.

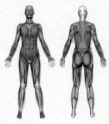

Modifications

Harder: Instead of jumping one foot straight forward, jump the foot diagonally forward so that it crosses under your torso. Then, jump the foot back to starting position. Repeat, alternating sides, to give your oblique muscles a challenging workout.

Level
· Beginner

Duration

· 2 minutes

Benefits
· Stabilizes core
· Strengthens glutes
  and quadriceps
· Improves
  coordination

Caution

· Pregnancy
· Lower-back issues

Annotation Key
Bold text indicates target muscles
Black text indicates other working muscles
* indicates deep muscles

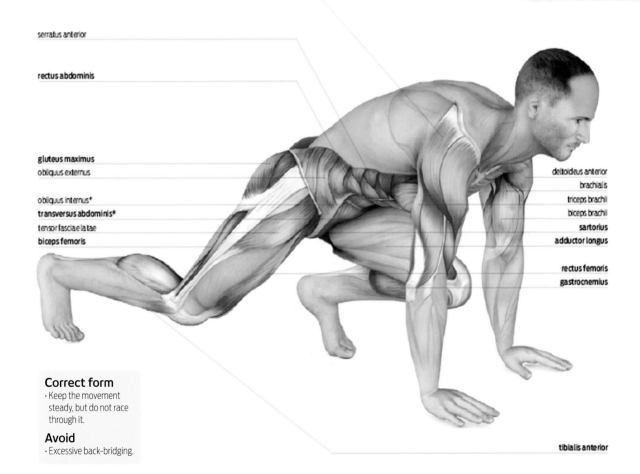

deltoideus posterior

serratus anterior

rectus abdominis

gluteus maximus
obliquus externus

obliquus internus*
transversus abdominis*
tensor fasciae latae
biceps femoris

deltoideus anterior
brachialis
triceps brachii
biceps brachii
sartorius
adductor longus

rectus femoris
gastrocnemius

tibialis anterior

Correct form
· Keep the movement
  steady, but do not race
  through it.

Avoid
· Excessive back-bridging.

Body-Weight Squat

Body-Weight Squat is a full-body exercise. Completing it correctly means using your core properly. It may look like an easy move, but there is more to it: as well as engaging your leg muscles, it engages nearly every muscle in your lower body. Perfecting this exercise is a great way to combat the weakness that often develops from a sedentary lifestyle.

1 Stand upright, with your feet shoulder-width apart and your arms outstretched in front of you.

2 Bend your legs and lower your body until your thighs are parallel to the floor, pushing your buttocks out slightly and maintaining a flat back.

3 Push through your heels back into an upright position

4 Repeat, working up to 3 sets of 15.

Correct form
· Keep your head up and your chest out so that your body forms a straight line.

Avoid
· Allowing your knees to hyperextend past your feet.

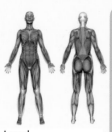

Annotation Key
Bold text indicates target muscles
Black text indicates other working muscles
* indicates deep muscles

Back View

gluteus maximus

semitendinosus

biceps femoris

semimembranosus

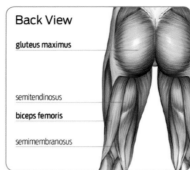

Level
· Beginner

Duration
· 3 minutes

Benefits
· Improves coordination
· Strengthens and tones glutes and quadriceps
· Helps maintain sound cardiovascular system

Caution
· Lower-back issues
· Knee issues

obliquus externus

gluteus medius*

transversus abdominis*

vastus intermedius*

adductor magnus

rectus femoris

vastus medialis

sartorius

tensor fasciae latae

vastus lateralis

gastrocnemius

tibialis anterior

soleus

abductor hallucis

Modifications

Easier: Place a fitness ball at the level of your upper back and lean against a wall. Follow the steps for Body-Weight Squat while keeping your back braced against the ball.

Medicine Ball Squat to Press

Medicine Ball Squat to Press works your entire body. A multifunctional exercise, it calls upon a spectrum of different muscles to engage at the same time.

1 Stand upright, holding the medicine ball in front of your chest. Plant your feet shoulder-width apart, and stick your buttocks slightly outward.

2 Lower toward the floor until your thighs are parallel to the floor.

Correct form
· Keep your head up and your chest out so your body forms a straight line.

Avoid
· Allowing your knees to hyperextend past your feet.

3 Push evenly through your heels to an upright position, and extend your arms overhead.

4 Lower your arms, assume the starting position, and repeat, completing 3 sets of 15.

Level
· Intermediate

Duration
· 3 minutes

Benefits
· Improves coordination
· Strengthens and tones glutes and quadriceps
· Helps maintain sound cardiovascular system

Caution
· Lower-back issues
· Knee issues

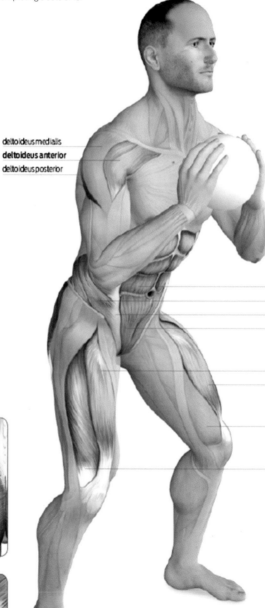

deltoideus medialis
deltoideus anterior
deltoideus posterior

rectus abdominis
obliquus externus
obliquus internus*
transversus abdominis*

vastus intermedius*
rectus femoris

vastus medialis

vastus lateralis

Back View

gluteus minimus
gluteus medius*

gluteus maximus

Front View

serratus anterior

Annotation Key
Bold text indicates target muscles
Black text indicates other working muscles
* indicates deep muscles

Balance Push-Up

Balance Push-Up is an advanced upper-body exercise. To complete it correctly demands proper stabilization of your core.

1 Assume a push-up position with your hands balanced on a fitness ball, shoulder-width apart.

2 Keeping your body in one straight line, bend your arms and lower your chest until it is nearly touching the fitness ball.

3 Straighten your arms, pushing to full extension.

4 Repeat, aiming for 3 sets of 10.

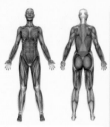

Correct form
· Keep your hands planted on the ball.
· Try to keep the ball as still as possible.
· Keep your heels lifted so that you are
  balancing on your toes.

Avoid
· Arching your back.
· Rushing through the movement.

Annotation Key
Bold text indicates target muscles
Black text indicates other working muscles
* indicates deep muscles

Front View

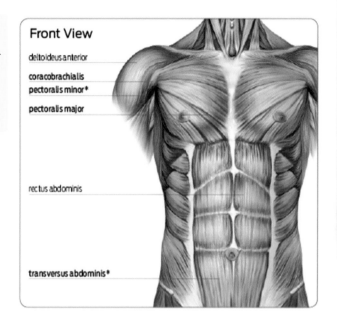

deltoideus anterior

coracobrachialis

pectoralis minor*

pectoralis major

rectus abdominis

transversus abdominis*

Level
· Advanced

Duration
· 3 minutes

Benefits
· Builds upper-body
  strength and stability
· Stabilizes spine
  and core

Caution
· Lower-back pain
· Wrist pain
· Shoulder issues

rhomboideus*

trapezius

triceps brachii

obliquus internus*

obliquus externus

vastus intermedius*

rectus femoris

Kneel on Ball

Kneel on Ball really challenges your core stability. Before attempting this advanced exercise solo, it is best to try it out with a fitness partner guiding you while you find your balance. Once balanced, fully engage your core and concentrate on keeping the ball as still as possible while your partner spots you.

1 Stand upright with a fitness ball in front of you.

2 Place one knee on top of the ball, and then slowly place the other one on the ball as well. Ask a partner to hold your torso in place while you find your balance.

3 Remain balanced for 15 seconds, stretching your arms out to your sides. Release.

4 Repeat, working up to 3 sets of 30-second balances.

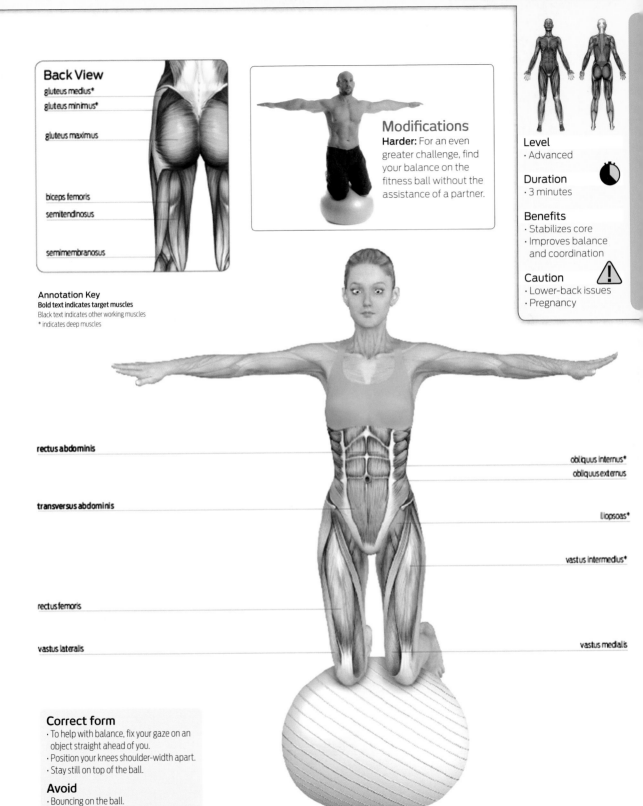

Back View

- gluteus medius*
- gluteus minimus*
- gluteus maximus
- biceps femoris
- semitendinosus
- semimembranosus

Annotation Key
Bold text indicates target muscles
Black text indicates other working muscles
* indicates deep muscles

Modifications

Harder: For an even greater challenge, find your balance on the fitness ball without the assistance of a partner.

Level
· Advanced

Duration
· 3 minutes

Benefits
· Stabilizes core
· Improves balance and coordination

Caution
· Lower-back issues
· Pregnancy

- rectus abdominis
- transversus abdominis
- rectus femoris
- vastus lateralis
- obliquus internus*
- obliquus externus
- iliopsoas*
- vastus intermedius*
- vastus medialis

Correct form
· To help with balance, fix your gaze on an object straight ahead of you.
· Position your knees shoulder-width apart.
· Stay still on top of the ball.

Avoid
· Bouncing on the ball.

Medicine Ball Over-the-Shoulder Throw

As simple as it may look, Medicine Ball Over-the-Shoulder Throw trains multiple muscles at once. It is a multipurpose exercise that helps you develop coordination, balance, and power while working on core stability and strength.

1 Stand upright, with a medicine ball in your hands, held low with your arms extended. Rotate your core, moving your extended arms slightly upward and to the side so that the medicine ball follows your body's twist.

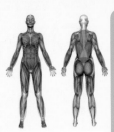

Annotation Key
Bold text indicates target muscles
Black text indicates other working muscles
* indicates deep muscles

Correct form
· Follow through with your swing.
· Bend your legs slightly as you twist.
· Follow the ball with your gaze.

Avoid
· Rushing through the movement.

2 Twist your torso in the other direction as you raise your arms in an arc. At the top of the arc, with your torso twisted, release the ball to your partner.

3 Lower your arms and return your torso to center.

4 Repeat. Perform 15 repetitions, and then switch sides, working up to 3 sets of 15 repetitions per side.

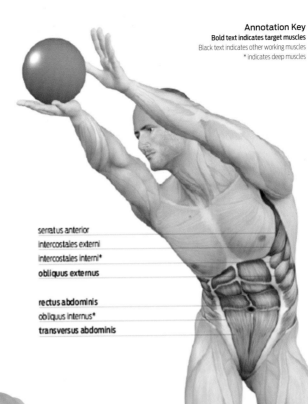

serratus anterior

intercostales externi

intercostales interni*

obliquus externus

rectus abdominis

obliquus internus*

transversus abdominis

Level
· Beginner

Duration
· 3 minutes

Benefits
· Stabilizes core
· Improves balance and coordination
· Strengthens shoulders and upper back

Caution
· Lower-back issues
· Rotator cuff injury

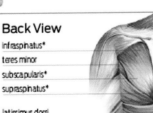

Back View
infraspinatus*

teres minor

subscapularis*

supraspinatus*

latissimus dorsi

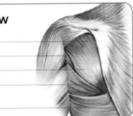

Fitness Ball Split Squat

Fitness Ball Split Squat is an advanced leg exercise. But it doesn't just involve your legs: to perform it correctly requires drawing upon a sound core so that your whole body gets a workout.

1 Stand with a fitness ball behind you. Place your hands on your hips.

2 Bend one leg to rest your ankle and the top of your foot on the ball.

3 Bend the knee of your front leg until the thigh is nearly parallel to the floor while simultaneously bending your back leg.

4 Straighten both legs to return to a standing position. Repeat to perform 15 repetitions. Switch legs and repeat, building up to 3 sets of 15 per leg.

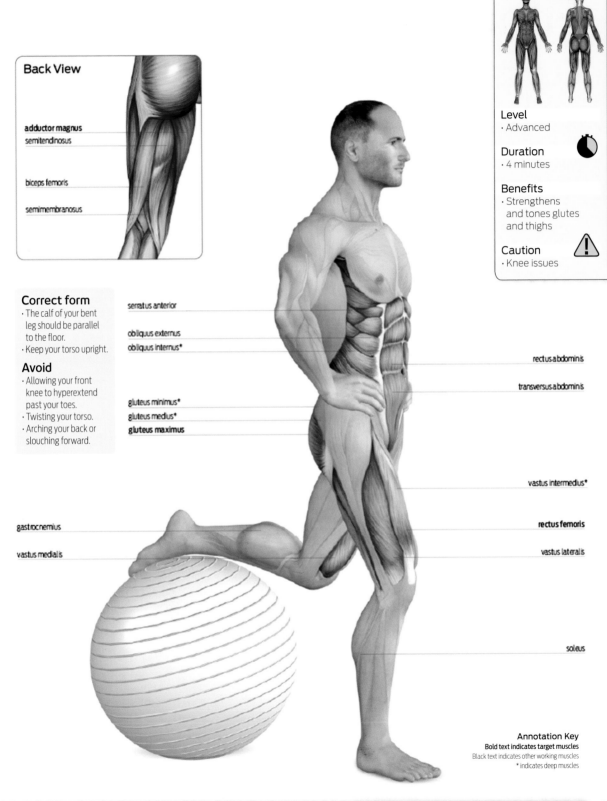

Back View

adductor magnus

semitendinosus

biceps femoris

semimembranosus

Level
· Advanced

Duration
· 4 minutes

Benefits
· Strengthens and tones glutes and thighs

Caution
· Knee issues

Correct form
· The calf of your bent leg should be parallel to the floor.
· Keep your torso upright.

Avoid
· Allowing your front knee to hyperextend past your toes.
· Twisting your torso.
· Arching your back or slouching forward.

serratus anterior

obliquus externus

obliquus internus*

gluteus minimus*

gluteus medius*

gluteus maximus

gastrocnemius

vastus medialis

rectus abdominis

transversus abdominis

vastus intermedius*

rectus femoris

vastus lateralis

soleus

Annotation Key
Bold text indicates target muscles
Black text indicates other working muscles
* indicates deep muscles

Fitness Ball Prone Row to External Rotation

Fitness Ball Prone Row to External Rotation is an advanced exercise that challenges your rotator cuffs and upper back. It also effectively works your core. This exercise is best preceded by a thorough warm-up to loosen your shoulder girdle.

1 Begin facedown on top of a fitness ball, with your torso supported. Balance on your toes, with your legs separated for stability.

2 Bend your arms to form 90-degree angles, with your upper arms parallel to the floor.

3 Pull your arms back as high as possible into a rowing position.

4 Rotate your forearms until they are parallel to the floor.

5 Reverse the movement until your fingers are nearly touching the floor.

6 Repeat to perform 3 sets of 15.

Level
· Advanced

Duration
· 3 minutes

Benefits
· Strengthens shoulders and upper back
· Improves balance and posture

Caution
· Lower-back issues
· Rotator cuff injury

Back View
infraspinatus*
teres minor
subscapularis*
supraspinatus*
latissimus dorsi

Front View
rectus abdominis
obliquus internus*
transversus abdominis

rhomboideus*

latissimus dorsi

obliquus externus

Correct form
· Remain as stable as possible on top of the ball.
· Keep your fingers active and outstretched.

Avoid
· Hyperextending your back.
· Allowing one or both feet to lift off the floor.
· Straining your neck by trying to look up.

Annotation Key
Bold text indicates target muscles
Black text indicates other working muscles
* indicates deep muscles

Fitness Ball Seated External Rotation

Fitness Ball Seated External Rotation targets your upper back and shoulders, particularly your rotator cuff muscles, in addition to the muscles of your core.

1 Sit on top of the fitness ball, with one foot firmly planted on the floor and the other slightly raised.

2 In your left hand, grasp a light dumbbell, and then rest your elbow on your raised knee. Position your left arm to hold the dumbbell against your chest, forearm level with the floor.

3 Rotate your left arm until your fist is pointing toward the ceiling.

4 Lower your left arm, and repeat to complete 15 repetitions.

5 Switch sides and repeat. Work up to performing 2 sets of 15.

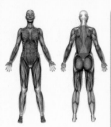

Annotation Key
Bold text indicates target muscles
Black text indicates other working muscles
* indicates deep muscles

Level
· Advanced

Duration
· 3 minutes

Benefits
· Strengthens
  shoulders and
  upper back
· Improves posture

Caution
· Rotator cuff injury

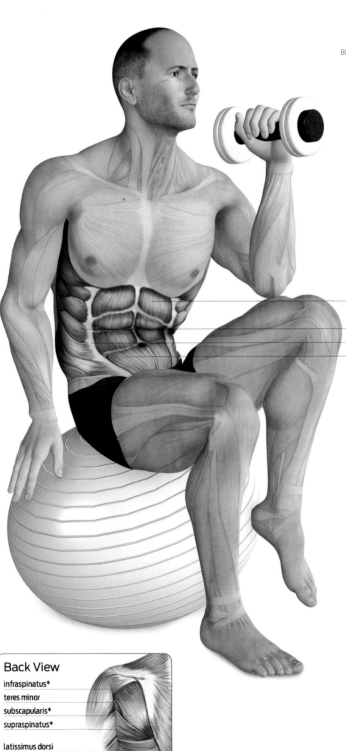

rectus abdominis

obliquus externus

obliquus internus*

transversus abdominis

Back View

infraspinatus*

teres minor

subscapularis*

supraspinatus*

latissimus dorsi

Correct form
· Remain balanced and stable on top
  of the fitness ball.
· Keep your resting arm by your hip for
  balance and support.
· Gaze forward.

Avoid
· Allowing the elbow of your working
  arm to slide off your knee.
· Shifting your weight on top of the ball.

Medicine Ball Walkover

Medicine Ball Walkover calls upon the major muscles of your upper body, challenging them to stay active and engaged as you carry out the movement.

1 Assume a push-up position, with your arms wider than shoulder-distance apart and the medicine ball under one hand.

2 Slowly bend both arms, lowering yourself toward the floor as if you were beginning a normal push-up.

3 Begin to straighten your arms as you raise your body toward starting position. Quickly pass the ball from one hand to the other.

4 Straighten your arms and raise your body back to starting position.

5 Repeat to complete 2 sets of 15.

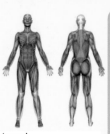

Level
· Advanced

Duration
· 2 minutes

Benefits
· Stabilizes core and upper body
· Tones arms
· Builds coordination

Caution
· Shoulder issues

rhomboideus*

triceps brachii

deltoideus anterior

pectoralis major

rectus abdominis

coracobrachialis

transversus abdominis

Correct form
· Keep your feet planted.
· Keep your body in one straight line.
· Keep your gaze downward.

Avoid
· Bouncing your body between repetitions.
· Straining your neck by trying to look forward.
· Rushing through the movement.

Fitness Ball Band Fly

Fitness Ball Band Fly is an excellent exercise for working your chest. Of course, this movement will also call your core into play.

1 Run an exercise band under your fitness ball. Lie back, with your upper back supported by the ball. With your arms extended out to your sides, hold one handle of the band in each hand.

2 Bend your arms slightly as you begin to contract your chest in a hugging motion.

3 Lengthen your arms to full extension until your chest is fully contracted.

4 Return to starting position and repeat, working up to 3 sets of 15.

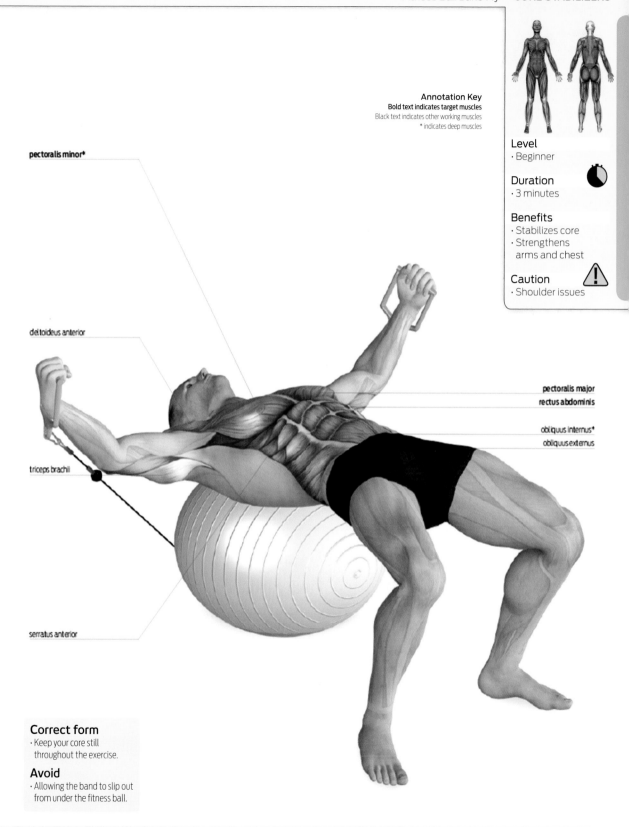

Annotation Key
Bold text indicates target muscles
Black text indicates other working muscles
* indicates deep muscles

pectoralis minor*

deltoideus anterior

pectoralis major

rectus abdominis

obliquus internus*

obliquus externus

triceps brachii

serratus anterior

Level
· Beginner

Duration
· 3 minutes

Benefits
· Stabilizes core
· Strengthens arms and chest

Caution
· Shoulder issues

Correct form
· Keep your core still throughout the exercise.

Avoid
· Allowing the band to slip out from under the fitness ball.

Fitness Ball Walk-Around

Fitness Ball Walk-Around offers a great challenge
for your core stability. It also works your arms
and sharpens your sense of balance.

1 Assume a push-up position, with your shins
resting on top of the fitness ball.

2 One at a time, "walk" your hands to the side and
turn your body so that it rotates in a half circle.

3 Walk your hands in the reverse direction,
returning your body to starting position.

Correct form
· Keep the fitness ball as still and stable as possible.
· Keep your legs, torso, and neck in a straight line.
· Keep your gaze downward.
· Keep your hands' "steps" small enough that you
  can control the movement.

Avoid
· Twisting your body.
· Straining your neck by trying to look forward.
· Rushing through the movement.

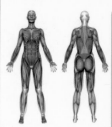

4 Repeat, completing 3 half circles in one direction and then 3 in the other.

Level
· Advanced

Duration
· 3 minutes

Benefits
· Strengthens shoulders and abdominals
· Stabilizes core
· Develops balance and coordination

Caution
· Shoulder issues
· Wrist pain
· Lower-back pain

Front View

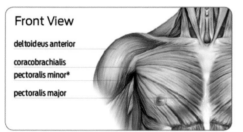

deltoideus anterior

coracobrachialis

pectoralis minor*

pectoralis major

Annotation Key
Bold text indicates target muscles
Black text indicates other working muscles
* indicates deep muscles

vastus intermedius*

quadratus lumborum*

latissimus dorsi

erector spinae*

rectus femoris

soleus

tibialis anterior

trapezius

deltoideus medialis

deltoideus posterior

vastus lateralis

vastus medialis

tensor fasciae latae

iliopsoas*

transversus abdominis*

serratus anterior

rectus abdominis

Medicine Ball Pullover on Fitness Ball

Medicine Ball Pullover on Fitness Ball is great for working the latissimus dorsi. The latissimus dorsi, often just called the "lats," is the largest of the back muscles and engages any time you pull something, such as when you open a door.

1 Lie on top of a fitness ball with your head supported and your feet shoulder-width apart. Grasp a medicine ball in your hands.

2 Extend your arms to hold the medicine ball above your chest.

Correct form
· Perform the movement slowly and with control.

Avoid
· Rushing through the movement.
· Locking your arms when you bring the ball behind your head.

3 Bend your arms as you bring the ball behind your head.

4 Lengthen your arms as you raise the ball back above your chest.

5 Repeat, completing 3 sets of 15.

Level
· Intermediate

Duration
· 3 minutes

Benefits
· Strengthens the large muscles of your back
· Stabilizes upper body

Caution
· Shoulder issues

Back View

levator scapulae*

deltoideus posterior

teres major

rhomboideus*

pectoralis minor*

obliquus internus*

triceps brachii

pectoralis major

latissimus dorsi

Annotation Key
Bold text indicates target muscles
Black text indicates other working muscles
* indicates deep muscles

Side Lunge and Press

Side Lunge and Press is a combo exercise that works both your upper and lower body. The lunge to the side develops the often-neglected adductors and abductors, as well as your core, and the press works out your shoulders.

Correct form
· Ease into the lunge.
· Keep your torso stable and upright.

Avoid
· Rushing through the movement.

1 Stand upright, holding a dumbbell in each hand.

2 Raise both dumbbells over your head, arms straight.

3 Bend your right leg as you lunge to the right side. At the same time, bend your right arm to lower the dumbbell to just above shoulder height.

4 Raise the arm, and return your bent leg to center. Repeat on the other side, working up 3 sets of 15 repetitions per side.

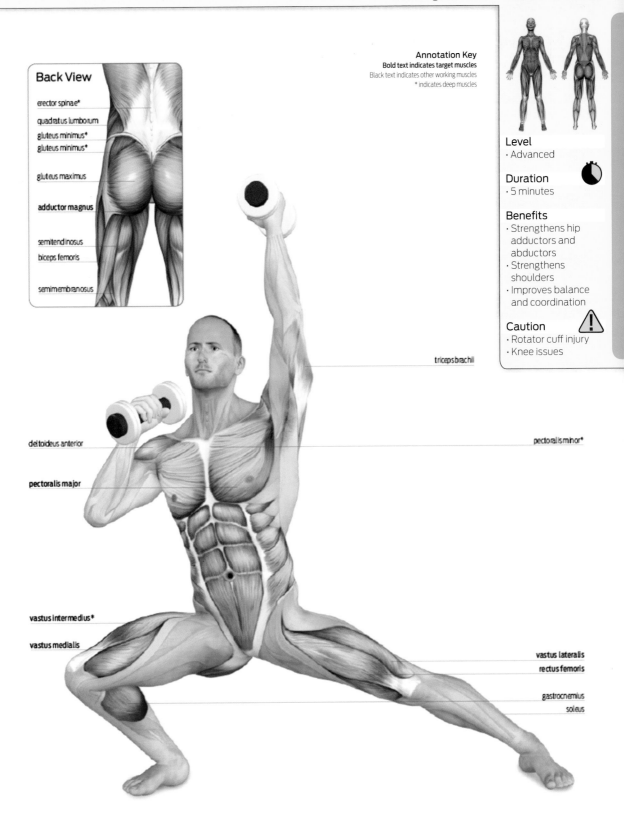

Back View

erector spinae*

quadratus lumborum

gluteus minimus*

gluteus minimus*

gluteus maximus

adductor magnus

semitendinosus

biceps femoris

semimembranosus

Annotation Key
Bold text indicates target muscles
Black text indicates other working muscles
* indicates deep muscles

Level
· Advanced

Duration
· 5 minutes

Benefits
· Strengthens hip
  adductors and
  abductors
· Strengthens
  shoulders
· Improves balance
  and coordination

Caution
· Rotator cuff injury
· Knee issues

triceps brachii

deltoideus anterior

pectoralis major

vastus intermedius*

vastus medialis

pectoralis minor*

vastus lateralis

rectus femoris

gastrocnemius

soleus

Hip Crossover

Hip Crossover effectively targets your lower-back and oblique muscles. As with many core exercises, when executing Hip Crossover, aim for controlled movements. You want your muscles—not momentum—to move you.

1 Lie on your back with your arms lengthened away from your body and your legs bent at a 90-degree angle and lifted off the floor.

2 Brace your abs, and lower your knees to the side, dropping them as close to the floor as possible without lifting your shoulders off the floor.

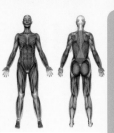

3 Return to the starting position, hold for a moment, and then repeat on the other side. Work up to 15 repetitions per side.

Level
· Intermediate

Duration
· 3 minutes

Benefits
· Stabilizes core
· Tones abs

Caution
· Lower-back issues

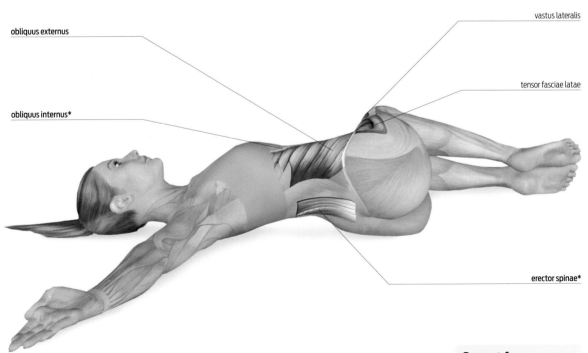

obliquus externus

obliquus internus*

vastus lateralis

tensor fasciae latae

erector spinae*

Correct form
· Keep your core centered.
· Move carefully and with control.

Avoid
· Excessively swinging your legs.

Annotation Key
Bold text indicates target muscles
Black text indicates other working muscles
* indicates deep muscles

Hip Raise

Adding movement to the traditional shoulder bridge, Hip Raise really challenges your core strength. It is not only an abdominal and lower-back exercise, but it targets your gluteal and hamstring muscles, too.

1 Lie on your back with your legs bent, your feet flat on the floor, and your arms along your sides.

2 Push through your heels while raising your pelvis until your torso is aligned with your thighs.

3 Lower and then repeat, working up to 3 sets of 15.

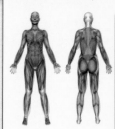

Back View

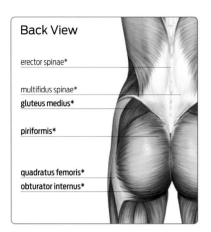

erector spinae*

multifidus spinae*
gluteus medius*

piriformis*

quadratus femoris*
obturator internus*

Correct form
· Push through your heels, not your toes.
· Roll your shoulders under once you are
  in the raised position.
· Tighten your thighs and buttocks.

Avoid
· Tucking you chin toward your chest.
· Overextending your abdominals past
  your thighs in the raised position.

Annotation Key
Bold text indicates target muscles
Black text indicates other working muscles
* indicates deep muscles

Level
· Beginner

Duration
· 3 minutes

Benefits
· Strengthens glutes
  and hamstrings
· Stretches chest
  and spine

Caution

· Lower-back issues
· Neck issues
· Shoulder issues

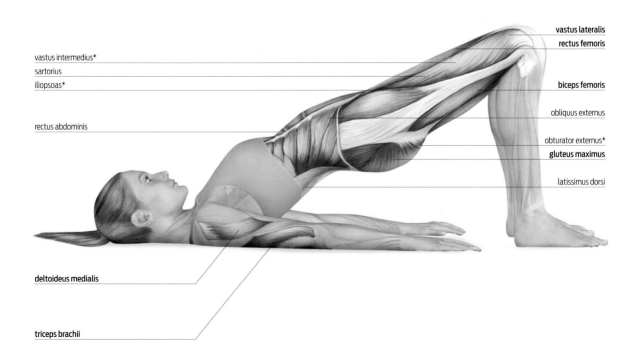

vastus intermedius*

sartorius

iliopsoas*

rectus abdominis

deltoideus medialis

triceps brachii

vastus lateralis
rectus femoris

biceps femoris

obliquus externus

obturator externus*
gluteus maximus

latissimus dorsi

Fitness Ball Hip Raise

Fitness Ball Hip Raise targets your core muscles, particularly the glutes. Along the way, your hamstrings get a great workout, too.

1 Lie on your back with your arms along your sides. Bend your knees, and rest your feet on the fitness ball.

2 Push through your heels while raising your pelvis until your torso is aligned with your thighs.

3 Lower and repeat, building up to for 3 sets of 15.

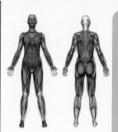

Modifications

Harder: Perform the exercise with one leg extended upward. Challenge yourself to keep your core stable—which requires a great deal of strength and control.

Front View

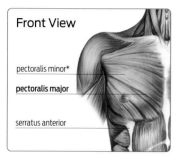

pectoralis minor*

pectoralis major

serratus anterior

Annotation Key
Bold text indicates target muscles
Black text indicates other working muscles
* indicates deep muscles

Level
· Intermediate

Duration
· 3 minutes

Benefits
· Strengthens glutes and hamstrings
· Stretches chest and spine

Caution
· Lower-back issues
· Neck issues
· Shoulder issues

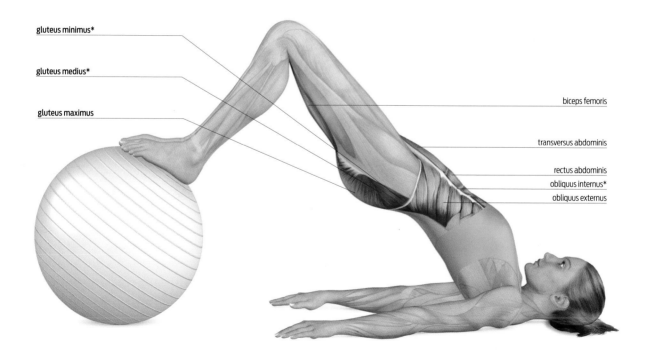

gluteus minimus*

gluteus medius*

gluteus maximus

biceps femoris

transversus abdominis

rectus abdominis
obliquus internus*
obliquus externus

Fitness Ball Bridge

Bridging exercises are great for toning the legs and buttocks. Fitness Ball Bridge adds another layer of challenge to this classic—working on an unstable ball means that you must keep your entire core fully engaged so that you maintain your balance.

1 Begin faceup, with your head, shoulders, and upper back supported by a fitness ball. Your feet should be planted shoulder-width apart or slightly wider, and your knees bent so that your buttocks are close to the floor. Place your hands on your hips.

2 Pushing through your heels, raise your torso until your upper body is parallel to the floor.

3 Lower to starting position. Repeat, aiming for 3 sets of 15.

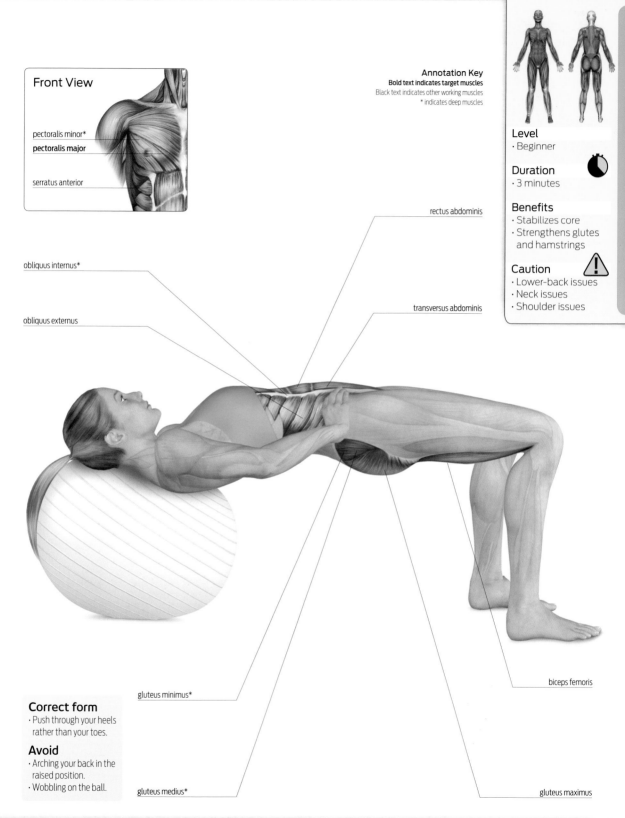

Annotation Key
Bold text indicates target muscles
Black text indicates other working muscles
* indicates deep muscles

Level
· Beginner

Duration
· 3 minutes

Benefits
· Stabilizes core
· Strengthens glutes
  and hamstrings

Caution
· Lower-back issues
· Neck issues
· Shoulder issues

Front View

pectoralis minor*

pectoralis major

serratus anterior

rectus abdominis

obliquus internus*

transversus abdominis

obliquus externus

biceps femoris

Correct form
· Push through your heels
  rather than your toes.

Avoid
· Arching your back in the
  raised position.
· Wobbling on the ball.

gluteus minimus*

gluteus medius*

gluteus maximus

Stiff-Legged Deadlift

Stiff-Legged Deadlift is a standard among body-builders who want to work their hamstrings. Add this exercise to your regimen, and you'll also target your glutes and the erector muscles in your back.

1 Hold a pair of dumbbells in front of your thighs, with your knees bent and your buttocks pushed out slightly.

2 Keeping your back flat, lower your dumbbells toward the floor.

3 Raise your torso as you bring the dumbbells slightly above your knees.

4 Repeat, building up to 3 sets of 15.

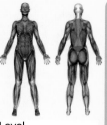

Correct form
· Keep your back flat throughout the exercise.
· Gaze forward.

Avoid
· Arching or rounding your back.
· Avoid standing completely up at the top to
 keep the tension on the hamstrings and glutes.

Level
· Intermediate

Duration
· 3 minutes

Benefits
· Stretches and
 strengthens
 hamstrings, glutes
 and back muscles
· Improves lower-
 body flexibility

Caution
· Lower-back issues

Annotation Key
Bold text indicates target muscles
Black text indicates other working muscles
* indicates deep muscles

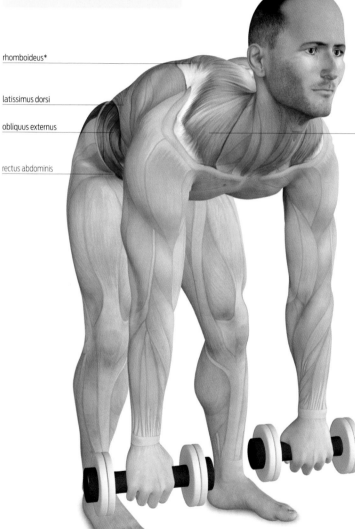

rhomboideus*

latissimus dorsi

obliquus externus

rectus abdominis

trapezius

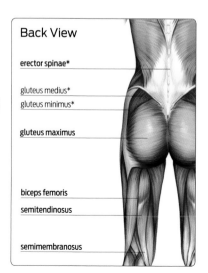

Back View

erector spinae*

gluteus medius*
gluteus minimus*

gluteus maximus

biceps femoris

semitendinosus

semimembranosus

Standing One-Legged Row

Standing One-Legged Row will greatly challenge the stabilization of your core, testing your balance and the functionality of your entire upper body. This exercise works your lats and arms, as well as your legs. Although it may seem difficult at first, with regular practice it will become easier as your core stability improves.

1 Stand upright, holding a dumbbell in your right hand.

2 Extend your right leg behind you. At the same time, lean forward, extending your left arm in front of you for balance and bending your left leg slightly.

Modifications
Easier: For help with balance, rest one arm on top of a fitness ball as you carry out the row.

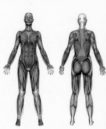

3 Bend your right elbow as you lift your weight upward into the row position.

4 Lower your right arm. Repeat the arm movement, performing 15 rows.

5 Return to the upright position and then repeat on the other side. Work up to 3 sets of 15 per arm.

Level
· Advanced

Duration
· 3 minutes

Benefits
· Strengthens and tones lats, arms, and legs
· Stabilizes core
· Improves balance

Caution
· Lower-back issues

Annotation Key
Bold text indicates target muscles
Black text indicates other working muscles
* indicates deep muscles

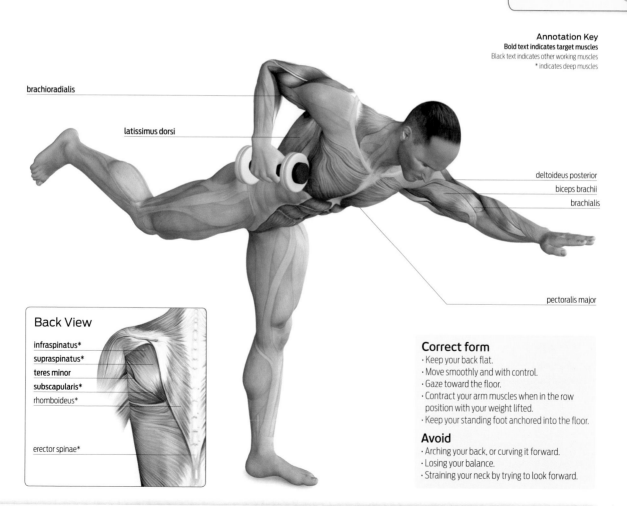

brachioradialis

latissimus dorsi

deltoideus posterior

biceps brachii

brachialis

pectoralis major

Back View
infraspinatus*
supraspinatus*
teres minor
subscapularis*
rhomboideus*

erector spinae*

Correct form
· Keep your back flat.
· Move smoothly and with control.
· Gaze toward the floor.
· Contract your arm muscles when in the row position with your weight lifted.
· Keep your standing foot anchored into the floor.

Avoid
· Arching your back, or curving it forward.
· Losing your balance.
· Straining your neck by trying to look forward.

Contents

Sit-Up 98

Rise and Reach 100

One-Armed Sit-Up 102

Medicine Ball Sit-Up 104

Crunch 106

Bicycle Crunch 108

Diagonal Crunch with
Medicine Ball 110

Fitness Ball Side Crunch 112

V-Up 114

Fitness Ball Crunch 116

Reverse Crunch 118

Big Circles with
Medicine Ball 120

Medicine Ball Slam 122

Kneeling Crunch with Band 124

One-Armed Band Pull 126

Penguin Crunch 128

Wood Chop with Band 130

Wood Chop
with Fitness Ball 132

Medicine Ball Standing
Russian Twist 134

Fitness Ball Seated
Russian Twist 136

Fitness Ball Russian Twist 138

Fitness Ball Alternating
Leg Tuck .140

Leg Raise .142

Side Leg Raise 144

Body Saw .146

Side Bend .148

Vertical Leg Crunch 150

Band Roll-Down
with Twist .152

Good Mornings 154

Superman .156

Let's be honest: many of us work out because we want to look better, whether it means fitting into a smaller jeans size, unveiling visibly defined abs at the beach, or "just" sporting that much-coveted toned appearance.

Strengthening the core, that muscular power station at the center of the body, is a remarkably effective way to do just that. Along the way, you will also feel better: slimmer, stronger, and more powerful. Mix and match from the following exercises to suit your fitness goals. For instance, Fitness Ball Side Crunch, performed regularly, will help you achieve to-die-for obliques, while the simple Sit-Up, performed correctly, will really tone those abdominals.

Core Strengtheners

Sit-Up

No core-training regimen would be complete without the Sit-Up. This workout staple is effective for both strengthening and defining the abdominal muscles, and it works your hip flexors, too. Form is crucial—to avoid stressing your spine and/or the muscles in your head and neck, make sure that your abdominals are driving the movement.

1 Lie on your back, with your legs bent and your feet planted on the floor. Bend your arms, and place your hands behind your head so that your elbows flare outward.

2 Engage your abdominals as you raise your shoulders and torso.

3 With control, lower your shoulders and torso back to starting position.

4 Repeat. Work up to 3 sets of 20.

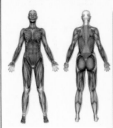

Annotation Key
Bold text indicates target muscles
Black text indicates other working muscles
* indicates deep muscles

Correct form
· Lead with your abdominals, not with your neck.
· Keep your feet planted on the floor.
· Keep the movement slow and controlled.

Avoid
· Relying on momentum to move up or down.
· Using your neck or lower back to drive the movement.
· Twisting your neck, torso, or hips.

Level
· Beginner

Duration
· 3 minutes

Benefits
· Strengthens abs
· Stabilizes core

Caution
· Lower-back issues
· Neck issues

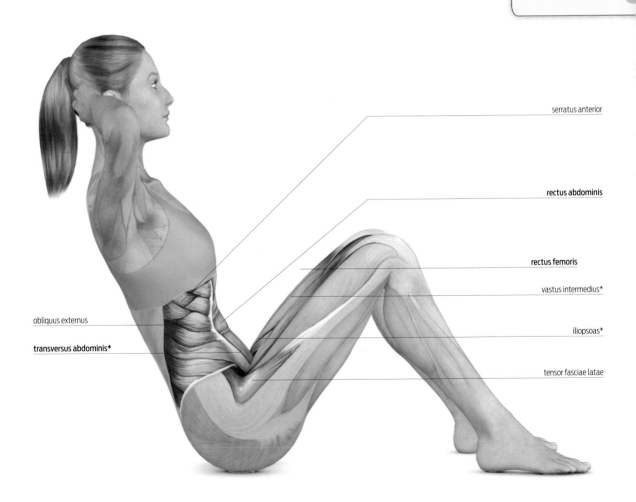

serratus anterior

rectus abdominis

rectus femoris

vastus intermedius*

iliopsoas*

tensor fasciae latae

obliquus externus

transversus abdominis*

Rise and Reach

Rise and Reach is a simple exercise, yet it is highly effective for both strengthening and defining your abdominal muscles while also working your hip flexors. Practicing proper form will protect your spine, as well as the muscles in your head and neck, from any stress or strain.

1 Lie on your back with your legs bent and your feet firmly planted on the floor. Extend your arms straight along your sides.

2 Lift your shoulders, head, and neck slightly off the floor.

3 Using your abdominal muscles to drive the movement, raise your upper torso off the floor toward your legs.

4 Lower and repeat, working up to 3 sets of 20.

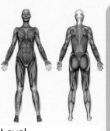

Correct form
· Lead with your abdominals, not with your neck.
· Keep your feet planted on the floor.

Avoid
· Using excessive momentum.
· Overusing your lower back.

Front View

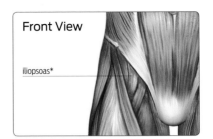

iliopsoas*

Level
· Beginner

Duration
· 3 minutes

Benefits
· Strengthens abs
· Stabilizes core

Caution
· Lower-back issues
· Neck issues

Annotation Key
Bold text indicates target muscles
Black text indicates other working muscles
* indicates deep muscles

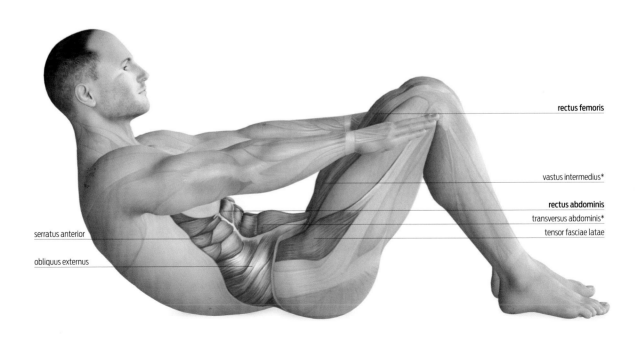

rectus femoris

vastus intermedius*

rectus abdominis
transversus abdominis*
tensor fasciae latae

serratus anterior

obliquus externus

One-Armed Sit-Up

One-Armed Sit-Up is a challenging twist
on the traditional Sit-Up, engaging the
obliques and the latissimus dorsi, as well
as the rectus abdominis.

1 Lie on your back, with your left leg bent
and your right leg extended along the floor.
Extend your left arm behind your head, and rest
your right arm along your side.

2 Pushing through your left heel, raise your
shoulders and torso off the floor until you
are sitting nearly upright and your left arm is
directly over your head.

3 Gradually lower to the floor.

Correct form
· Anchor the foot of your bent leg into the floor.
· Draw upon your core muscles to drive the movement.
· Keep your extended arm as straight as possible.

Avoid
· Relying on momentum to sit up or down.
· Using your neck or lower back to drive the movement.
· Twisting your neck, torso, or hips.

4 Repeat, working up to 15. Switch sides and repeat, aiming for 2 sets of 15 on both sides.

Level
· Advanced

Duration
· 3 minutes

Benefits
· Strengthens abdominals
· Stabilizes core

Caution
· Lower-back issues
· Neck issues

Annotation Key
Bold text indicates target muscles
Black text indicates other working muscles
* indicates deep muscles

deltoideus posterior

vastus medialis

triceps brachii
rectus abdominis
brachialis
latissimus dorsi

adductor longus
transversus abdominis*
vastus intermedius*
rectus femoris

pectineus*
tensor fasciae latae

vastus lateralis
extensor digitorum
flexor digitorum*

Medicine Ball Sit-Up

Medicine Ball Sit-Up takes a basic exercise one step further. By grasping the medicine ball throughout the exercise, your arms are unable to propel you upward. As a result, your abdominals have to work extra hard—reaping greater benefits in the process.

1 Lie on your back with your legs bent and your feet firmly planted on the floor. Grasp a medicine ball between your hands and hold it just in front of your chest.

2 Raise your shoulders and torso off the floor toward your legs.

3 Lower and repeat, working up to 3 sets of 20.

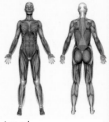

Correct form
· Lead with your abdominals, not with your neck.
· Keep your feet planted on the floor.
· Keep the medicine ball in front of your chest
  throughout all stages of the exercise.

Avoid
· Using excessive momentum.
· Overusing your lower back.

Annotation Key
Bold text indicates target muscles
Black text indicates other working muscles
*indicates deep muscles

Level
· Intermediate

Duration
· 3 minutes

Benefits
· Strengthens abs
· Stabilizes core

Caution
· Lower-back issues
· Neck issues

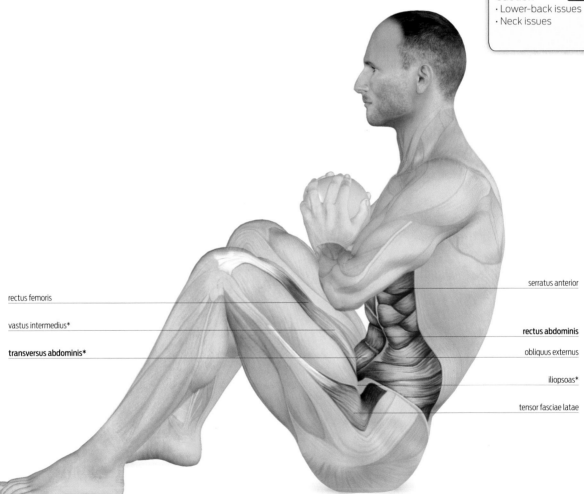

rectus femoris

vastus intermedius*

transversus abdominis*

serratus anterior

rectus abdominis

obliquus externus

iliopsoas*

tensor fasciae latae

Crunch

Like the Sit-Up, the Crunch is highly effective for isolating the rectus abdominis. Unlike the Sit-Up, however, your lower back never leaves the floor during the movement, which places less strain on the lumbar region of your spine. Lead with your abdominals, as if a string were hoisting you up by your belly button.

1 Lie on your back with your legs bent, elbows flared, and palms next to your ears.

2 Raise your head and shoulders off the floor while contracting your abdominals.

3 Lower and repeat, working up to 3 sets of 25 repetitions.

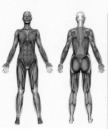

Front View

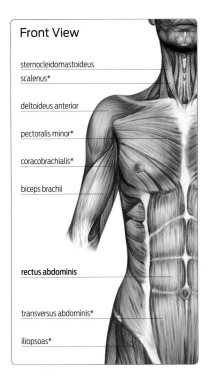

sternocleidomastoideus

scalenus*

deltoideus anterior

pectoralis minor*

coracobrachialis*

biceps brachii

rectus abdominis

transversus abdominis*

iliopsoas*

Correct form
· Keep both feet planted on the floor.
· Use your abs to drive the movement.

Avoid
· Overusing your neck.

Back View

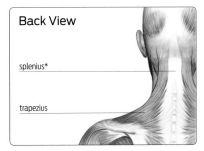

splenius*

trapezius

Annotation Key
Bold text indicates target muscles
Black text indicates other working muscles
* indicates deep muscles

Level
· Beginner

Duration

· 3 minutes

Benefits
· Strengthens abs
· Stabilizes core

Caution
· Lower-back issues
· Neck issues

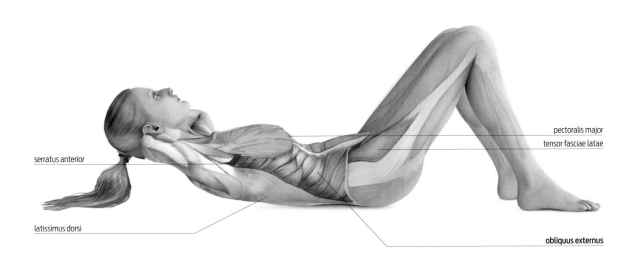

serratus anterior

latissimus dorsi

pectoralis major

tensor fasciae latae

obliquus externus

Bicycle Crunch

Bicycle Crunch is particularly effective for strengthening and toning your upper abdominals as well as your oblique muscles. Although you may be tempted to "cycle" quickly, perform each crunch smoothly and with control for best results.

1 Lie on your back with fingers at your ears, your elbows flared outward and your legs bent to form a 90-degree angle.

2 Begin to lift your shoulders and upper torso off the floor as your raise your right elbow diagonally. At the same time, bring your left knee toward your elbow and extend your right leg diagonally forward—until your right elbow and left knee meet.

Modifications
Easier: Bend both knees and place both feet on the floor, keeping them anchored there throughout the exercise. Leading with your abdominals, raise your entire torso off the floor as you bring your left elbow to your right knee. Lower and repeat, alternating sides.

Correct form
- Raise your elbow and opposite knee equally, so that they meet in the middle.

Avoid
- Raising your lower back off the floor.
- Rushing through the movement.

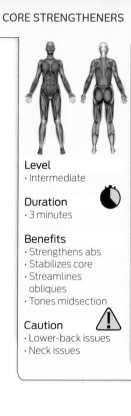

3 Lower, and then repeat on the other side. Alternating, repeat to perform 3 sets of 15 on both sides.

Level
· Intermediate

Duration
· 3 minutes

Benefits
· Strengthens abs
· Stabilizes core
· Streamlines obliques
· Tones midsection

Caution
· Lower-back issues
· Neck issues

Front View

rectus abdominis
obliquus externus

iliopsoas*
sartorius

adductor magnus
vastus intermedius*
rectus femoris

Annotation Key
Bold text indicates target muscles
Black text indicates other working muscles
* indicates deep muscles

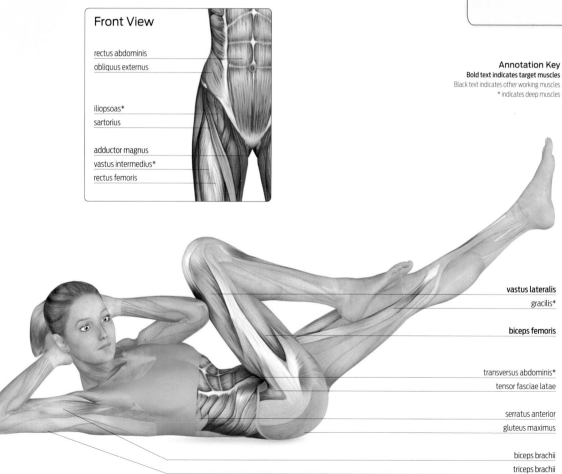

vastus lateralis
gracilis*

biceps femoris

transversus abdominis*
tensor fasciae latae

serratus anterior
gluteus maximus

biceps brachii
triceps brachii

Diagonal Crunch with Medicine Ball

Diagonal Crunch with Medicine Ball strengthens your abdominal, oblique, and intercostal muscles. You will notice the sides of your core getting tighter and stronger through regularly practicing this challenging move.

1 Holding a medicine ball in both hands, lie on your back with your arms and legs extended behind and in front of you, respectively, so that your body forms one straight line. Your legs should be shoulder-width apart.

2 Using your abdominals to drive the movement, move your arms and torso to one side.

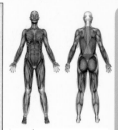

3 Bring your torso to an upright position with the ball planted in between your legs.

4 Lower back to starting position, with the medicine ball held flat on the floor over your head. Repeat on the other side. Work up to completing 3 sets of 15 repetitions per side.

Level
· Advanced

Duration
· 3 minutes

Benefits
· Strengthens abs
· Stabilizes core
· Streamlines obliques
· Tones midsection

Caution
· Lower-back issues
· Neck issues

Annotation Key
Bold text indicates target muscles
Black text indicates other working muscles
* indicates deep muscles

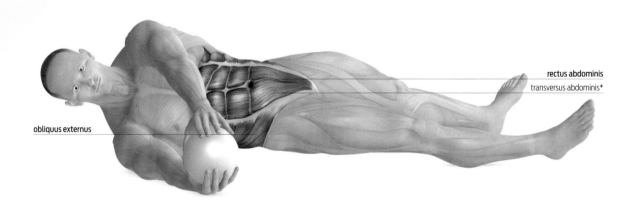

rectus abdominis

transversus abdominis*

obliquus externus

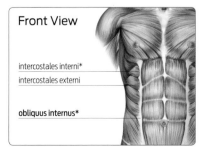

Front View

intercostales interni*

intercostales externi

obliquus internus*

Correct form
· Keep your legs and feet stable.
· Move smoothly and with control.
· Use your abdominal muscles to drive the movement.

Avoid
· Lifting your legs or feet off the floor.
· Jerking your upper body.

Fitness Ball Side Crunch

Fitness Ball Side Crunch is an advanced core-strengthening exercise. It is especially beneficial to your oblique and intercostal muscles.

1 Lie on your left side on top of a fitness ball, with your left hip and the left side of your torso supported by the ball. Bend both knees. Raise your left heel off the floor. Bring your right leg over your left, and rest your right foot in front of your left thigh. Place your fingertips on your ears with your elbows flared outward.

2 Using your abdominals to drive the movement, raise your torso until it is nearly upright.

3 Lower and repeat, building up to 15. Repeat on the other side. Aim for 3 sets of 15 per side.

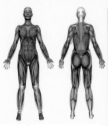

Correct form

· Aim to keep the fitness ball as stable as possible by maintaining your body position.
· Keep your arms in place.
· Keep your core strongly engaged.
· If desired, rest your back foot against a wall for help with balancing.

Avoid

· Rushing through the exercise.
· Using your legs to drive the movement.
· Allowing the ball to wobble.

Annotation Key
Bold text indicates target muscles
Black text indicates other working muscles
* indicates deep muscles

Level
· Advanced

Duration
· 3 minutes

Benefits
· Strengthens core
· Tones midsection, especially obliques

Caution
· Lower-back issues

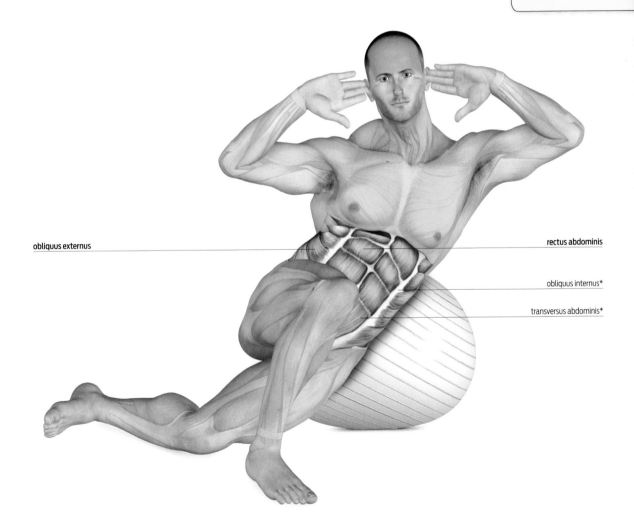

obliquus externus

rectus abdominis

obliquus internus*

transversus abdominis*

V-Up

The challenging V-Up targets both your upper and lower rectus abdominis, as it moves through its entire range of motion. Performing V-Ups is also an efficient way to strengthen your lower-back muscles and tighten your quads.

1 Lie on your back with your legs straight and your arms extended behind your head.

2 Simultaneously raise your arms and legs so that your fingertips are nearly touching your feet, while maintaining a flat back.

3 Lower and repeat, working up to 3 sets of 20 repetitions.

Modifications
Harder: Grasp a medicine ball in your hands, keeping it in place throughout the exercise.

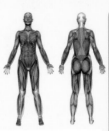

Front View

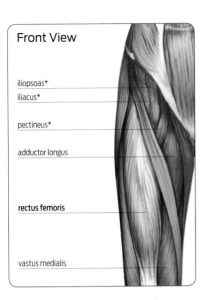

iliopsoas*

iliacus*

pectineus*

adductor longus

rectus femoris

vastus medialis

Correct form
· Keep your arms and legs straight.

Avoid
· Using a jerking motion as your raise or lower your arms and legs.

Annotation Key
Bold text indicates target muscles
Black text indicates other working muscles
* indicates deep muscles

Level
· Advanced

Duration
· 3 minutes

Benefits
· Strengthens core
· Increases spinal mobility

Caution
· Lower-back issues
· Neck issues

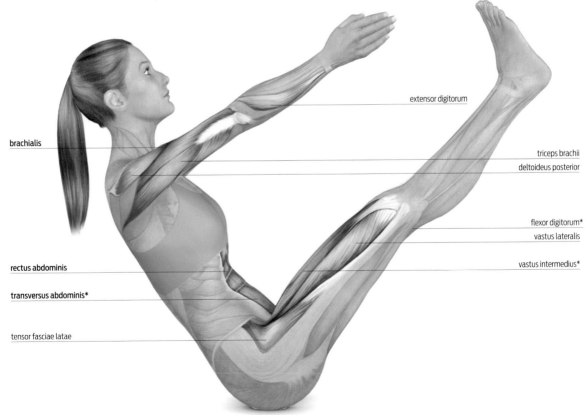

brachialis

extensor digitorum

triceps brachii

deltoideus posterior

flexor digitorum*

vastus lateralis

vastus intermedius*

rectus abdominis

transversus abdominis*

tensor fasciae latae

Fitness Ball Crunch

Fitness Ball Crunch adds a new dimension to the basic crunch exercise. By positioning yourself on top of the ball, you challenge your abs to work harder: as they work to drive the crunching movement, they also must stay engaged as you balance on top of the ball, trying not to let it wobble.

1 Lie on your back, with your feet planted wider than shoulder-distance apart, your back supported on the ball, your hands at your ears, and your elbows flared outward.

2 Simultaneously raise your arms and legs so that your arms are nearly touching your feet, while maintaining a flat back.

3 Lower and repeat, working up to 3 sets of 20.

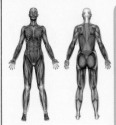

Annotation Key
Bold text indicates target muscles
Black text indicates other working muscles
* indicates deep muscles

Correct form
· Keep your legs anchored into the floor.
· Keep your lower back supported.
· Keep your body as stable as possible on top of the ball.

Avoid
· Allowing the ball to wobble.

Level
· Intermediate

Duration
· 3 minutes

Benefits
· Strengthens abs
· Stabilizes core

Caution
· Lower-back issues
· Neck issues

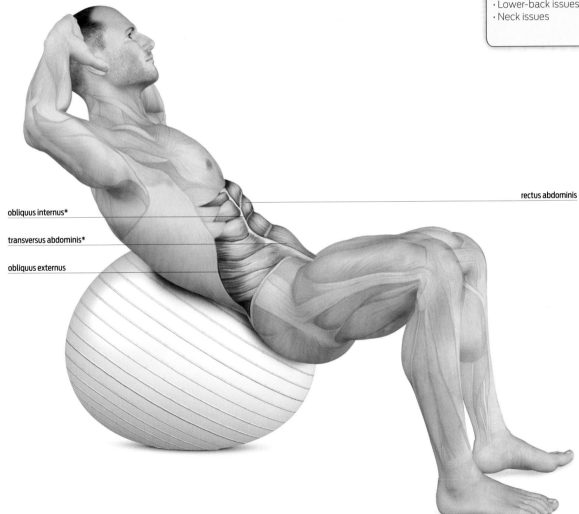

rectus abdominis

obliquus internus*

transversus abdominis*

obliquus externus

Reverse Crunch

Reverse Crunch is highly effective for isolating the lowest portion of the rectus abdominis, where most abdominal fat tends to be stored. Less is more with this exercise: your movements should be small but focused.

1 Lie on your back with your arms at your sides and your legs bent at a 90-degree angle with your feet off the floor.

2 Lift your buttocks a few inches off the mat as you bring your knees toward your chest.

3 Lower in a controlled manner. Repeat, working up to 3 sets of 20.

Front View

rectus abdominis

transversus abdominis*

iliopsoas*

sartorius

pectineus*

adductor longus

gracilis*

vastus medialis

Annotation Key
Bold text indicates target muscles
Black text indicates other working muscles
* indicates deep muscles

Correct form
· Lift with your abdominals rather than your neck or back.

Avoid
· Using excessive momentum.

Level
· Intermediate

Duration
· 3 minutes

Benefits
· Strengthens core and pelvic stabilizers
· Streamlines and defines lower abs

Caution
· Lower-back issues
· Neck pain
· Shoulder issues

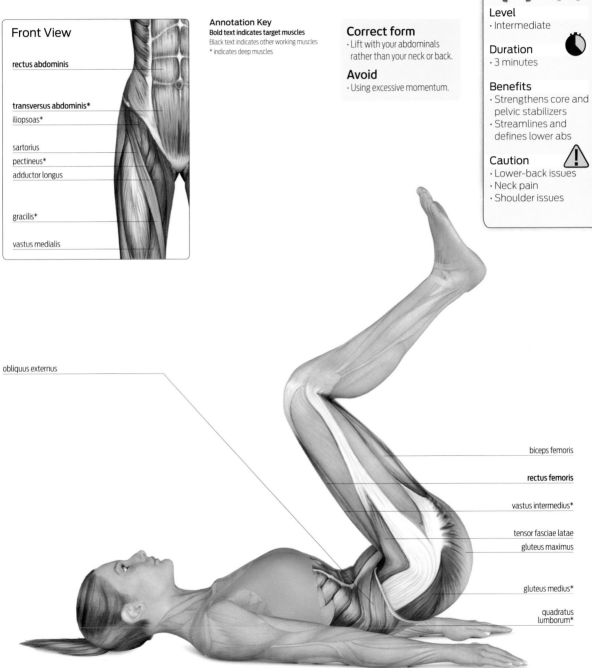

obliquus externus

biceps femoris

rectus femoris

vastus intermedius*

tensor fasciae latae

gluteus maximus

gluteus medius*

quadratus lumborum*

Big Circles with Medicine Ball

Big Circles with Medicine Ball are highly effective for working the front of your core. Here the muscles stay engaged as they move through their range of motion.

1 Stand with your feet planted shoulder-distance or slightly wider apart and a medicine ball grasped in both hands. Lift your arms overhead.

2 Continuing the circular movement, bring your arms out to the side, turning your head to follow the ball's movement with your gaze.

3 Keeping your arms extended, continue the circular movement to bring your arms down in front of you. Again, follow the ball's movement with your gaze.

4 Bring your arms to the opposite side.

5 Bring your arms overhead to starting position. Complete 30 circles, then repeat in the opposite direction for another 30.

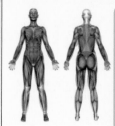

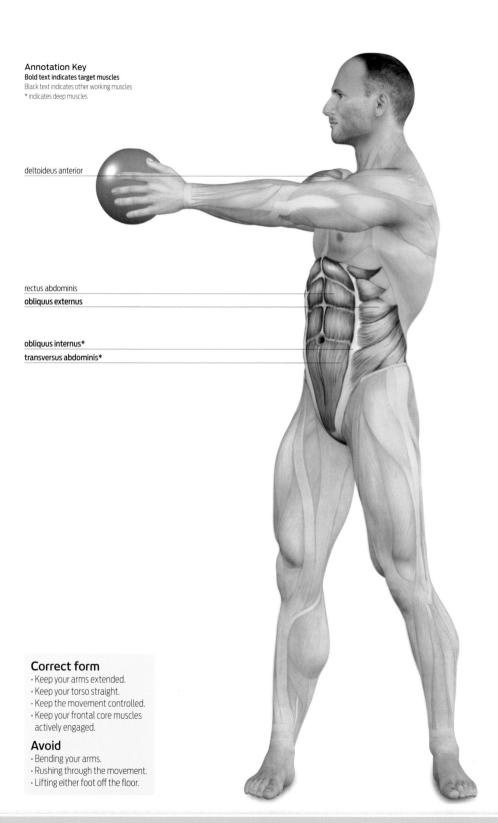

Annotation Key
Bold text indicates target muscles
Black text indicates other working muscles
* indicates deep muscles

deltoideus anterior

rectus abdominis
obliquus externus

obliquus internus*
transversus abdominis*

Level
· Beginner

Duration
· 6-12 minutes

Benefits
· Streamlines and
  defines abs

Caution

· Lower-back issues
· Shoulder issues

Correct form
· Keep your arms extended.
· Keep your torso straight.
· Keep the movement controlled.
· Keep your frontal core muscles
  actively engaged.

Avoid
· Bending your arms.
· Rushing through the movement.
· Lifting either foot off the floor.

Medicine Ball Slam

When performing Medicine Ball Slam with proper form, you will really feel the muscles of your shoulders working hard. Although this exercise is dynamic, do not get carried away and neglect your core muscles; they should stay strongly engaged throughout.

1 Stand with your feet planted shoulder-distance or slightly wider apart and a medicine ball grasped in both hands. Lift your arms overhead.

2 Keeping your back as straight as possible, bend your knees and stick your buttocks slightly outward as you bring the medicine ball down to shoulder height.

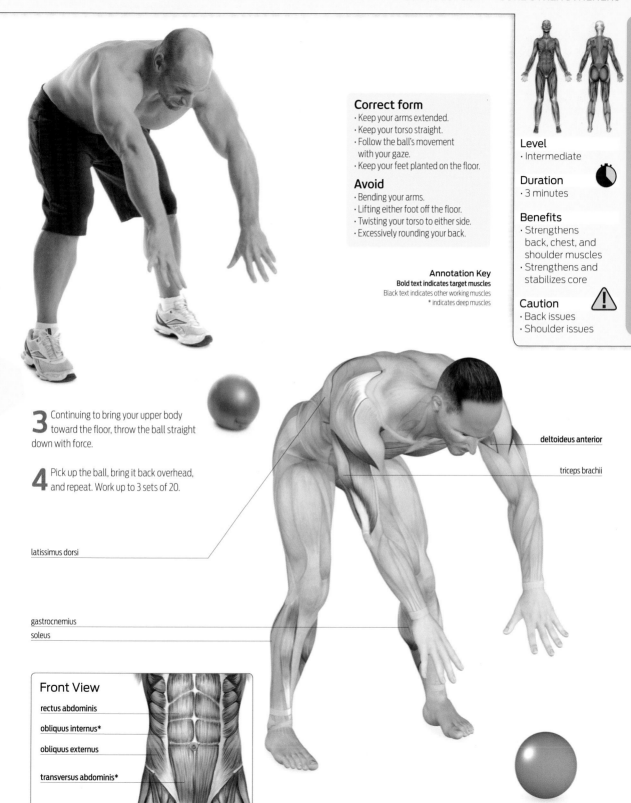

Correct form
· Keep your arms extended.
· Keep your torso straight.
· Follow the ball's movement
  with your gaze.
· Keep your feet planted on the floor.

Avoid
· Bending your arms.
· Lifting either foot off the floor.
· Twisting your torso to either side.
· Excessively rounding your back.

Annotation Key
Bold text indicates target muscles
Black text indicates other working muscles
* indicates deep muscles

Level
· Intermediate

Duration
· 3 minutes

Benefits
· Strengthens
  back, chest, and
  shoulder muscles
· Strengthens and
  stabilizes core

Caution
· Back issues
· Shoulder issues

3 Continuing to bring your upper body
toward the floor, throw the ball straight
down with force.

4 Pick up the ball, bring it back overhead,
and repeat. Work up to 3 sets of 20.

deltoideus anterior

triceps brachii

latissimus dorsi

gastrocnemius

soleus

Front View
rectus abdominis

obliquus internus*

obliquus externus

transversus abdominis*

Kneeling Crunch with Band

Kneeling Crunch with Band utilizes a resistance band to help engage and strengthen your core muscles. Form is crucial; to reap the greatest benefit, use your abs to drive the movement while keeping the rest of your body stable and aligned. To protect your knees, be sure to use a mat.

1 Loop a resistance band around a nearby stable object, and grasp the handles in both hands. Kneel on your mat, with your heels lifted. Bend your elbows and place the handles next to your ears.

2 Engaging your abdominals, bend forward from the hips until your torso is fully contracted.

3 Rise back to starting position. Repeat, building up to 3 sets of 25.

Correct form
· Keep your hands beside your ears.
· Keep your torso straight.
· Keep your abdominals strongly engaged.

Avoid
· Excessively rounding your back.
· Twisting your torso to either side.

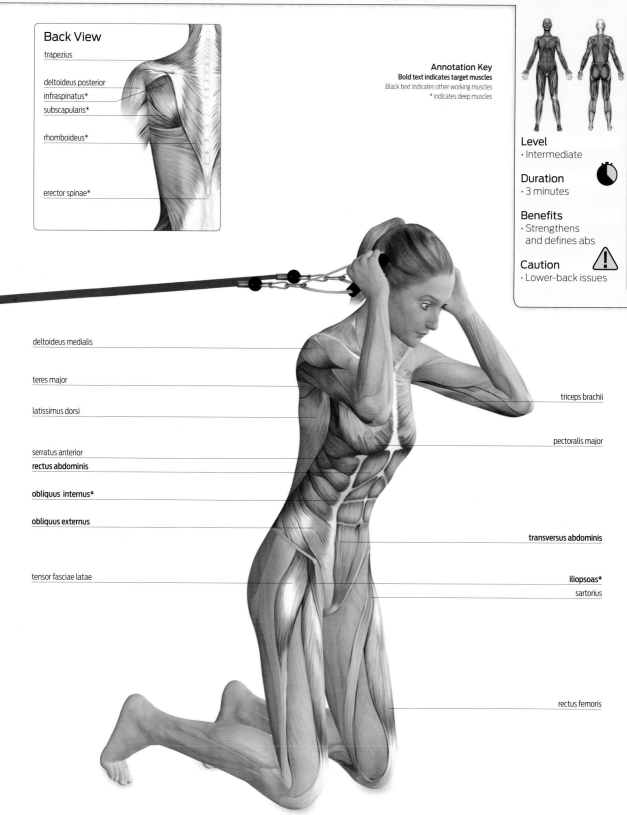

Back View

- trapezius
- deltoideus posterior
- infraspinatus*
- subscapularis*
- rhomboideus*
- erector spinae*

Annotation Key
Bold text indicates target muscles
Black text indicates other working muscles
* indicates deep muscles

Level
· Intermediate

Duration
· 3 minutes

Benefits
· Strengthens
 and defines abs

Caution
· Lower-back issues

- deltoideus medialis
- teres major
- latissimus dorsi
- serratus anterior
- **rectus abdominis**
- **obliquus internus***
- **obliquus externus**
- tensor fasciae latae

- triceps brachii
- pectoralis major
- **transversus abdominis**
- **iliopsoas***
- sartorius
- rectus femoris

One-Armed Band Pull

One-Armed Band Pull makes use of the resistance band to target the front of your core. The pull movement also benefits your back, particularly the latissimus dorsi.

1 Attach one end of a resistance band to a stable object, and grasp the other handle in one hand. Stand straight, with your feet planted shoulder-width apart, and extend the arm that is holding the band in front of you.

2 Bend your elbow as you bring the band toward your body in a rowing motion. Continue until the band is just below your chest.

3 Extend your arm back to starting position, and then repeat to perform 15 repetitions. Transfer the band to the other arm, and repeat, working up to 3 sets of 15 per side.

Correct form
· Keep your torso straight.
· Anchor your feet to the floor.

Avoid
· Twisting your torso.
· Rushing through the movement.

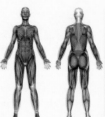

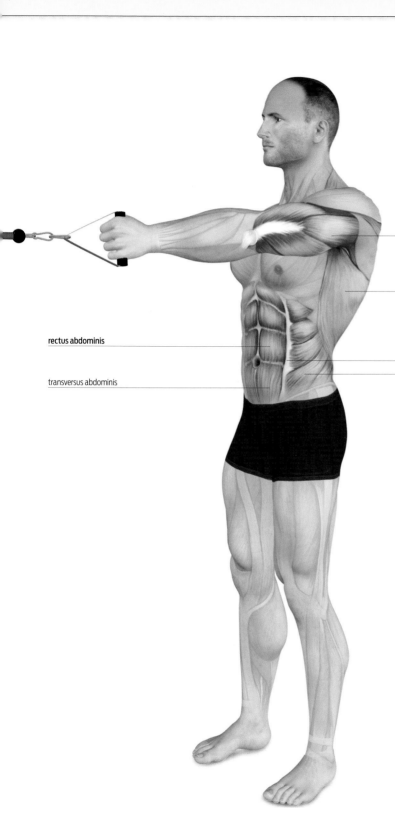

Level
· Beginner

Duration
· 3 minutes

Benefits
· Strengthens back
· Tones and defines abdominals

Caution
· Lower-back issues

triceps brachii

latissimus dorsi

rectus abdominis

obliquus internus*

obliquus externus

transversus abdominis

Annotation Key
Bold text indicates target muscles
Black text indicates other working muscles
* indicates deep muscles

Front View

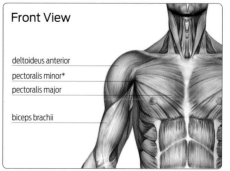

deltoideus anterior

pectoralis minor*

pectoralis major

biceps brachii

Penguin Crunch

Penguin Crunch, also called Penguin Heel Reach, targets your oblique muscles. Because it incorporates lateral movement of the abdominals, it is a great exercise to prepare you for any sport that requires rotational movement, such as swimming or diving.

1 Begin on your back, with your head elevated and your arms at your sides and raised off the floor.

2 Reach forward in a stabbing motion with one hand, and then pull back.

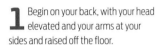

Correct form
· As you reach, pull in using your midsection.

Avoid
· Overusing your neck and/or back muscles.

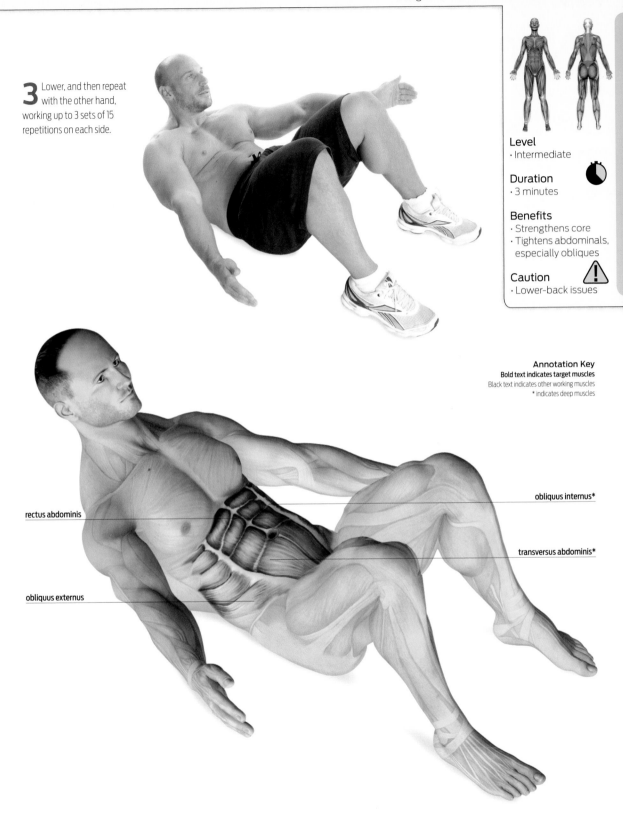

3 Lower, and then repeat with the other hand, working up to 3 sets of 15 repetitions on each side.

Level
· Intermediate

Duration
· 3 minutes

Benefits
· Strengthens core
· Tightens abdominals, especially obliques

Caution
· Lower-back issues

obliquus internus*

rectus abdominis

transversus abdominis*

obliquus externus

Wood Chop with Band

Wood Chop with Band is an effective exercise for strengthening your oblique muscles. Using the band adds an element of resistance to the movement, enhancing your results.

1 Attach one end of the band to a stable object. Stand straight while holding the other end of the band in both hands, your arms fully extended. Rotate your torso to one side, bringing the band with you.

2 Rotate to the other side, raising your arms as you turn. Feel your abdominals contract.

3 Lower your arms as you bring your torso back to center.

4 Repeat through the same range of motion on the other side, working up to 3 sets of 20 per side.

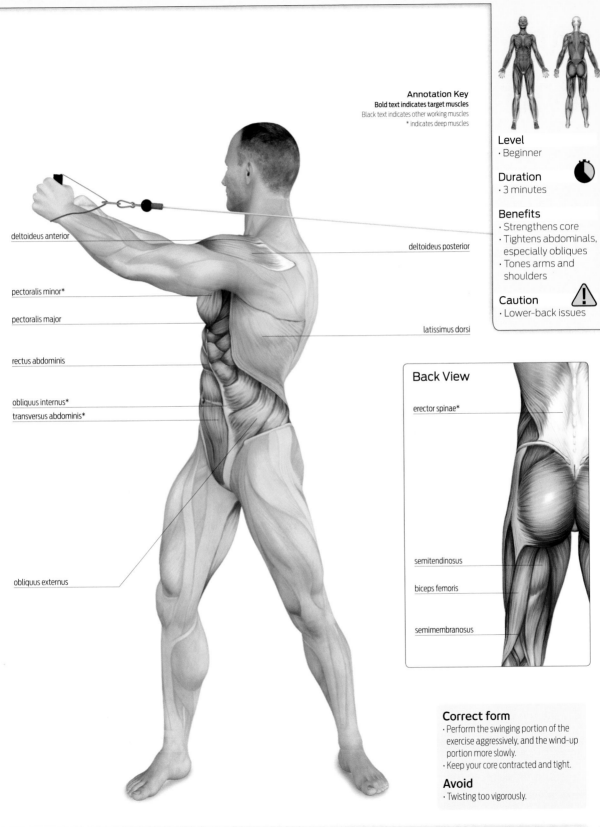

Annotation Key
Bold text indicates target muscles
Black text indicates other working muscles
* indicates deep muscles

Level
· Beginner

Duration
· 3 minutes

Benefits
· Strengthens core
· Tightens abdominals, especially obliques
· Tones arms and shoulders

Caution
· Lower-back issues

deltoideus anterior

deltoideus posterior

pectoralis minor*

pectoralis major

latissimus dorsi

rectus abdominis

obliquus internus*

transversus abdominis*

obliquus externus

Back View

erector spinae*

semitendinosus

biceps femoris

semimembranosus

Correct form
· Perform the swinging portion of the exercise aggressively, and the wind-up portion more slowly.
· Keep your core contracted and tight.

Avoid
· Twisting too vigorously.

Wood Chop with Fitness Ball

Wood Chop with Fitness Ball is another take on a gym classic. Perform this version of the Wood Chop to strengthen your abdominals, especially the oblique muscles. This exercise also works your arm and shoulder muscles.

1 Stand while holding a fitness ball, your arms fully extended. Rotate your torso to one side, bringing the ball with you.

2 Lower the ball across your body, and then follow through by rotating to the other side and raising the ball as you turn, as if swinging a baseball bat, while feeling your abdominals contract.

3 Lower the ball as you return your core to the center.

4 Repeat through the same range of motion on the other side, working up to 3 sets of 20 per side.

Correct form
· Perform the swinging portion of the exercise aggressively, and the wind-up portion more slowly.
· Keep your core contracted and tight.

Avoid
· Twisting too vigorously.

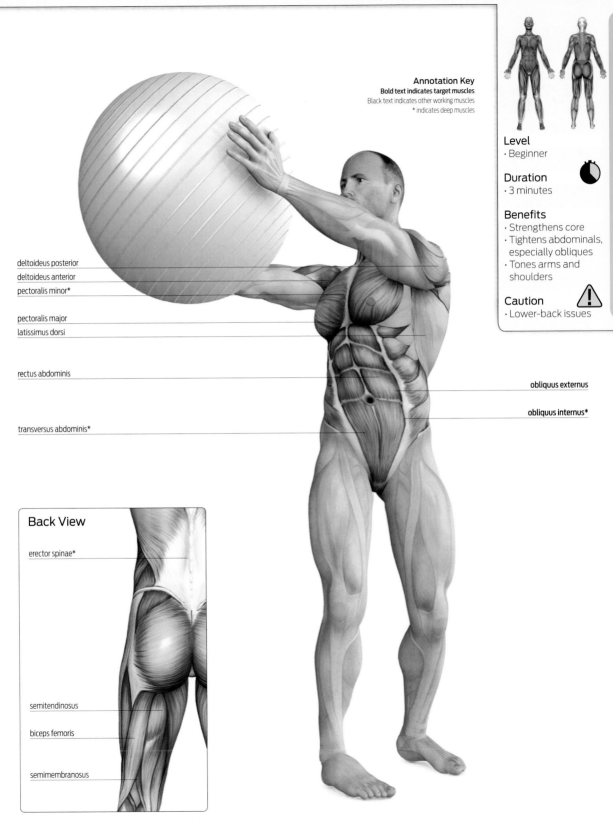

Annotation Key
Bold text indicates target muscles
Black text indicates other working muscles
* indicates deep muscles

Level
· Beginner

Duration
· 3 minutes

Benefits
· Strengthens core
· Tightens abdominals, especially obliques
· Tones arms and shoulders

Caution
· Lower-back issues

deltoideus posterior

deltoideus anterior

pectoralis minor*

pectoralis major

latissimus dorsi

rectus abdominis

transversus abdominis*

obliquus externus

obliquus internus*

Back View

erector spinae*

semitendinosus

biceps femoris

semimembranosus

Medicine Ball Standing Russian Twist

Medicine Ball Standing Russian Twist is an effective exercise for strengthening the major muscles of the your core. Challenge yourself to keep the rest of your body stable and aligned as you keep your core as active and engaged as possible.

1 Stand with your legs slightly wider than shoulder-distance apart. Keep your knees soft, bending them very slightly. Hold a medicine ball in front of you with arms extended.

2 Rotate your arms and torso to one side, back to center, and then to the other side.

3 Return to center and repeat, working up to 3 sets of 20 rotations.

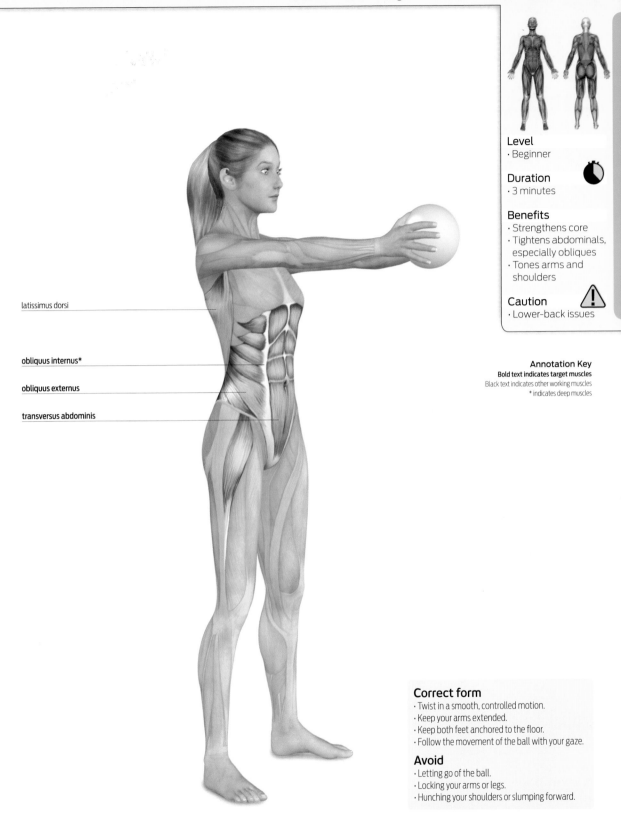

Level
· Beginner

Duration
· 3 minutes

Benefits
· Strengthens core
· Tightens abdominals, especially obliques
· Tones arms and shoulders

Caution
· Lower-back issues

Annotation Key
Bold text indicates target muscles
Black text indicates other working muscles
* indicates deep muscles

latissimus dorsi

obliquus internus*

obliquus externus

transversus abdominis

Correct form
· Twist in a smooth, controlled motion.
· Keep your arms extended.
· Keep both feet anchored to the floor.
· Follow the movement of the ball with your gaze.

Avoid
· Letting go of the ball.
· Locking your arms or legs.
· Hunching your shoulders or slumping forward.

Fitness Ball
Seated Russian Twist

Fitness Ball Seated Russian Twist is
effective for strengthening the major
muscles of your core, including your
obliques, lower-back extensors,
abdominals, and deep core stabilizers.

1 Sit with your legs apart while holding a
fitness ball at arm's length. Lean back
slightly to activate your core.

2 Rotate from side to side, keeping your back
as flat as possible.

Correct form
· Twist smoothly and with control.

Avoid
· Rounding your back.
· Rushing through the movement.

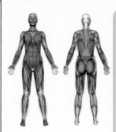

3 Work up to performing 3 sets of 20 rotations.

Level
· Intermediate

Duration
· 3 minutes

Benefits
· Strengthens core
· Tightens abdominals, especially obliques
· Tones arms and shoulders

Caution
· Lower-back issues

Annotation Key
Bold text indicates target muscles
Black text indicates other working muscles
* indicates deep muscles

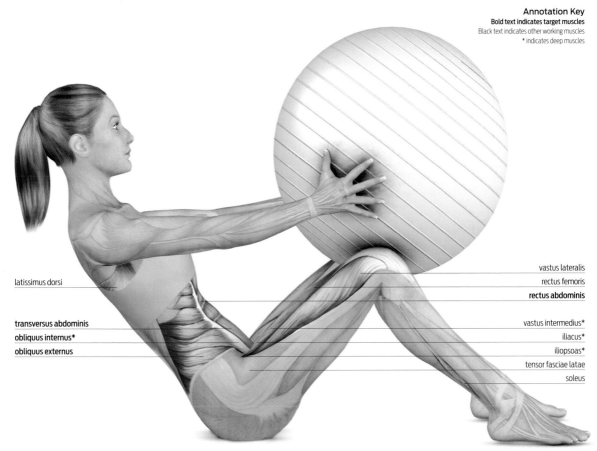

latissimus dorsi

transversus abdominis
obliquus internus*
obliquus externus

vastus lateralis
rectus femoris
rectus abdominis

vastus intermedius*
iliacus*
iliopsoas*
tensor fasciae latae
soleus

Fitness Ball Russian Twist

Fitness Ball Russian Twist offers a fun, unique way to strengthen your core—and whittle your waistline. It targets all of your abdominals, but because it incorporates rotation, it places an emphasis on the obliques.

1 Sit on your fitness ball, with feet planted shoulder-width apart. Roll forward until your neck is supported on the ball. Extend your arms to full lockout directly above your chest.

2 Turn one hip out to the side while also turning your torso and your arms.

3 Return to the center.

Correct form
· Move slowly and with control.

Avoid
· Allowing your upper back to hang off the fitness ball, unsupported.

4 Repeat to the other side, working up to 3 sets of 15 repetitions per side.

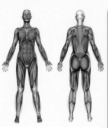

Level
· Intermediate

Duration
· 3 minutes

Benefits
· Strengthens core
· Tightens abdominals, especially obliques
· Tones arms and shoulders

Caution
· Lower-back issues

Annotation Key
Bold text indicates target muscles
Black text indicates other working muscles
* indicates deep muscles

Back View

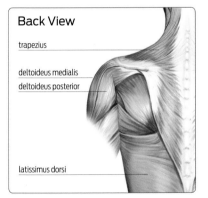

trapezius

deltoideus medialis
deltoideus posterior

latissimus dorsi

Front View

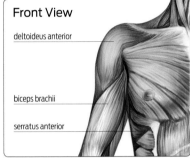

deltoideus anterior

biceps brachii

serratus anterior

rectus abdominis

transversus abdominis*
obliquus internus*
triceps brachii
obliquus externus

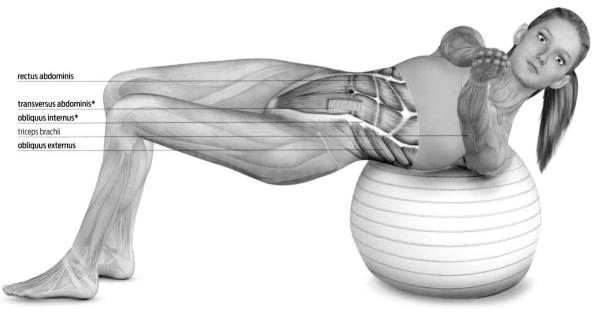

Fitness Ball Alternating Leg Tuck

Fitness Ball Alternating Leg Tuck is a powerful strengthener for your core. It benefits all of your powerhouse muscles, particularly targeting the lower abdominal area.

1 Sit upright on a fitness ball, with your feet planted in front of you, slightly wider than hip-distance apart, and your hands on the ball at your sides.

2 Raise one leg upward, bringing it toward your chest.

3 Lower the leg. Repeat on the other side, building up to 3 sets of 20 repetitions per leg.

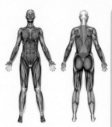

· Aim to touch your knee to your chest.
· Keep your torso and back straight.
· Maintain the bend in your knee as you raise your leg.
· Gaze forward.

Avoid
· Arching your back or curving it forward.

Annotation Key
Bold text indicates target muscles
Black text indicates other working muscles
* indicates deep muscles

Level
· Intermediate

Duration
· 4 minutes

Benefits
· Strengthens core
· Streamlines and defines abs

Caution
· Lower-back issues

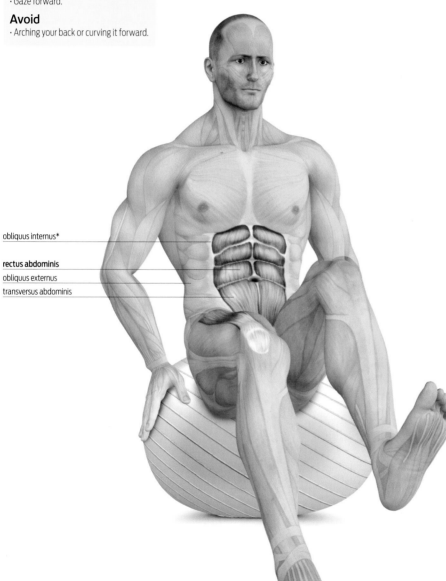

obliquus internus*

rectus abdominis

obliquus externus

transversus abdominis

Leg Raise

Leg Raise targets the transversus abdominis, that tough-to-reach lower abdominal area. This core-strengthener is easy to perform effectively, even for most beginners. Carry out this exercise regularly to see a reduction in abdominal fat.

Correct form
· Keep your upper body braced.
· Lift your legs back to starting position just as slowly as you lower them.

Avoid
· Using momentum, or your lower back, to drive the movement.

1 Lie on your back with your arms extended out to your sides.

2 Bend your legs slightly and elevate them off the floor.

3 Lower your legs to just above floor level, and then lift your legs back up.

4 Repeat, working up to 2 sets of 20.

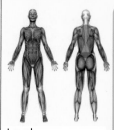

Front View

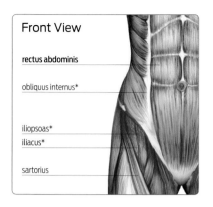

rectus abdominis

obliquus internus*

iliopsoas*

iliacus*

sartorius

Annotation Key
Bold text indicates target muscles
Black text indicates other working muscles
* indicates deep muscles

Modifications
Easier: Instead of raising both legs, raise one leg at a time.

Level
· Beginner

Duration
· 2 minutes

Benefits
· Strengthens core
· Streamlines and defines abs

Caution
· Lower-back issues

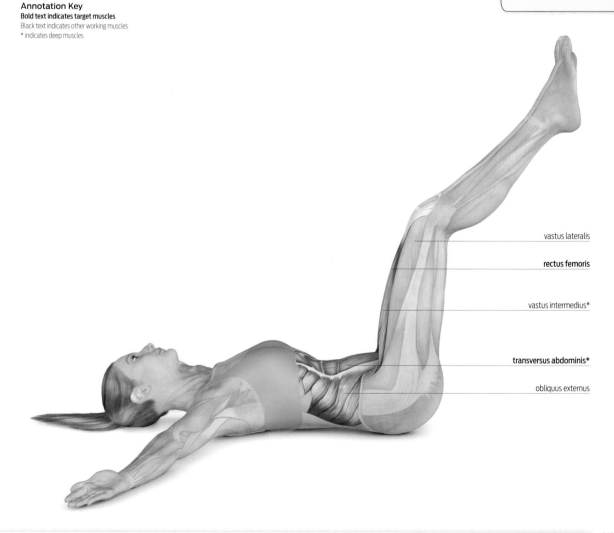

vastus lateralis

rectus femoris

vastus intermedius*

transversus abdominis*

obliquus externus

Side Leg Raise

Side Leg Raise is especially beneficial for your obliques and hip adductors. Concentrate on keeping the rest of your body still as you move your top leg a few inches up and then back down—moving with smooth control.

1 Begin on your side, with your legs stacked one on top of the other. Bend your bottom arm, brace your forearm against the floor, and place the hand of your top arm on your hip. Your torso should be raised off the floor, facing forward.

2 Raise your top leg a few inches.

3 Slowly lower the leg back to your starting position. Repeat to perform 20 raises. Switch sides and repeat, working up to 3 sets of 20 per side.

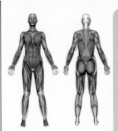

Back View

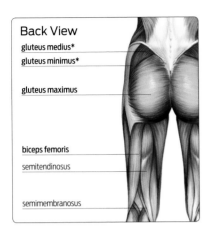

gluteus medius*

gluteus minimus*

gluteus maximus

biceps femoris

semitendinosus

semimembranosus

Annotation Key
Bold text indicates target muscles
Black text indicates other working muscles
* indicates deep muscles

Level
· Beginner

Duration
· 4 minutes

Benefits
· Strengthens core, especially obliques, and hip adductors

Caution

· Lower-back issues

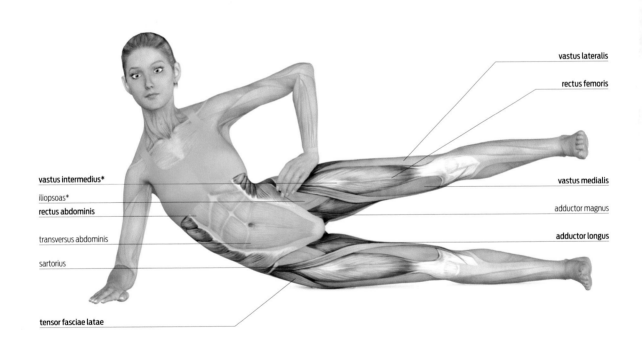

vastus lateralis

rectus femoris

vastus intermedius*

iliopsoas*

rectus abdominis

transversus abdominis

sartorius

tensor fasciae latae

vastus medialis

adductor magnus

adductor longus

Correct form
· Keep your top leg directly over your bottom leg throughout the exercise.
· Keep your torso straight.
· Keep your hips stacked.

Avoid
· Rushing through the movement.
· Tilting your top hip back or forward.

Body Saw

The core-strengthening Body Saw is harder than it looks. Challenge yourself to keep your body in a straight line as you shift back and forth like a saw. The better your form, the harder your abdominals and lower-back muscles will work.

1 Begin facedown, balancing on your toes and your forearms.

2 Shift your body backward, pressing into the floor with your forearms as you reposition your feet.

3 Shift your body forward to return to starting position. Repeat, working up to 3 sets of 20.

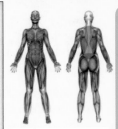

Annotation Key
Bold text indicates target muscles
Black text indicates other working muscles
* indicates deep muscles

Level
· Intermediate

Duration
· 3 minutes

Benefits
· Stabilizes core
· Strengthens abs

Caution
· Shoulder issues
· Lower-back issues

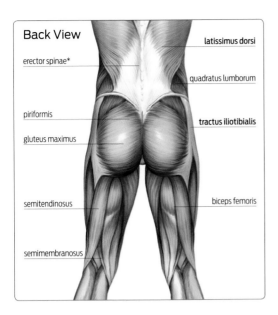

Back View

erector spinae*

latissimus dorsi

quadratus lumborum

piriformis

tractus iliotibialis

gluteus maximus

semitendinosus

biceps femoris

semimembranosus

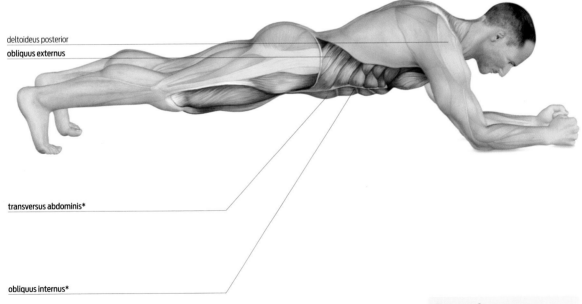

deltoideus posterior

obliquus externus

transversus abdominis*

obliquus internus*

Correct form
· Keep your body in one straight line.
· Gaze toward the floor.

Avoid
· Arching your back, or curving it forward.

Side Bend

Side Bend is a potent core-strengthening exercise that targets your oblique muscles. Lean only as far to the side as you can go while keeping your torso straight. If you find your torso twisting, this means your form needs to be corrected as your abdominals are not being challenged enough.

1 Stand with your feet planted shoulder-width apart and your arms at your sides.

2 Leading with your arm, lean over to one side while keeping your torso facing forward.

3 Engaging your abdominal muscles, lift your upper body back to center to stand tall.

4 Repeat on the other side. Alternating, work up to completing 3 sets of 20 per side.

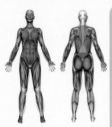

Correct form
· Gaze forward
· Keep both feet planted on the floor.

Avoid
· Avoid leaning forward or backward.
· Twisting your torso to either side.

Level
· Beginner

Duration
· 4 minutes

Benefits
· Strengthens and stretches obliques
· Tones midsection

Caution
· Lower-back issues

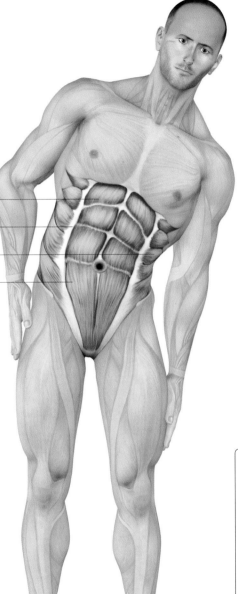

rectus abdominis

obliquus internus*

obliquus externus

transversus abdominis*

Annotation Key
Bold text indicates target muscles
Black text indicates other working muscles
* indicates deep muscles

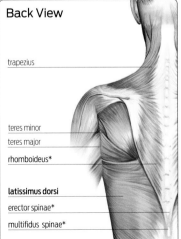

Back View

trapezius

teres minor

teres major

rhomboideus*

latissimus dorsi

erector spinae*

multifidus spinae*

Vertical Leg Crunch

When carrying out Vertical Leg Crunch, you should feel a strong sense that your abs are not just getting stronger but becoming streamlined and defined, too. With your legs up, your abdominals do almost all the work. Keep your movement smooth as you lower yourself to the floor, so that your core stays active throughout all stages of the exercise.

1 Lie on your back, with your arms extended behind your head and your legs extended in front of you so that your body forms one straight line.

2 Bring your arms over your head so they are reaching straight upward, your hands directly above your shoulders and your arms forming a 90-degree angle with the floor. Raise your legs until they are parallel to your arms.

3 Using your abdominals to drive the movement, lift your shoulders off the floor, reaching your extended fingers towards your toes.

4 Lower and repeat, aiming to carry out 3 sets of 20.

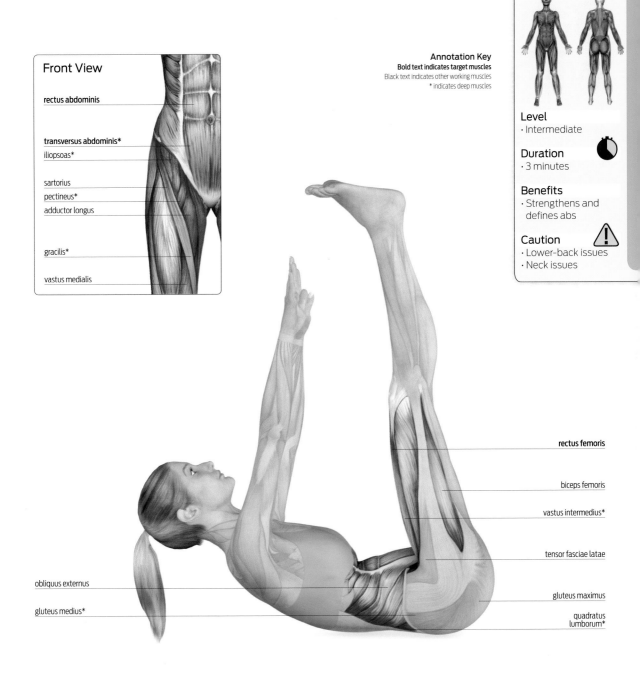

Front View

rectus abdominis

transversus abdominis*
iliopsoas*

sartorius
pectineus*
adductor longus

gracilis*

vastus medialis

Annotation Key
Bold text indicates target muscles
Black text indicates other working muscles
* indicates deep muscles

Level
· Intermediate

Duration
· 3 minutes

Benefits
· Strengthens and
defines abs

Caution
· Lower-back issues
· Neck issues

rectus femoris

biceps femoris

vastus intermedius*

tensor fasciae latae

gluteus maximus

quadratus
lumborum*

obliquus externus

gluteus medius*

Correct form
· Keep your arms and legs extended.
· Lower your upper back just as slowly as you raised it.
· Press your legs together as if they were a single leg.

Avoid
· Using your lower-back muscles to drive the movement.

Band Roll-Down with Twist

Thoroughly working your entire core, Band Roll-Down with Twist is a powerful strengthener. Although the movement may seem small, when performed correctly you will really feel its effects in your midsection.

1 Sit with your legs slightly bent, a resistance band looped beneath your heels. Grasp the handle with both hands and bring them to your ears.

2 Bring your elbows to your thighs as you contract your trunk, lowering your shoulders and upper back.

Correct form
- Elongate your upper body in starting position.
- Keep the handles of the resistance band next to your ears.
- Keep your legs and feet in place.

Avoid
- Rounding your back as you twist your torso to the side.

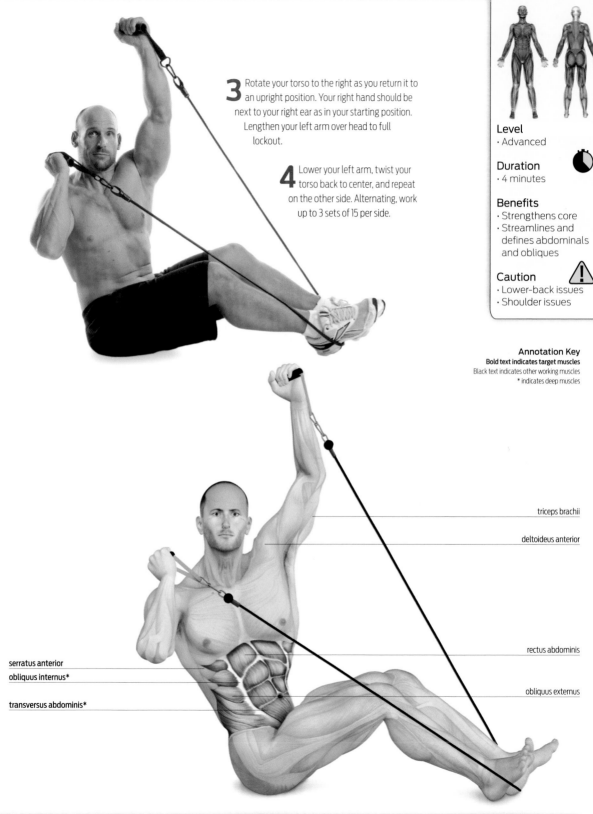

3 Rotate your torso to the right as you return it to an upright position. Your right hand should be next to your right ear as in your starting position. Lengthen your left arm over head to full lockout.

4 Lower your left arm, twist your torso back to center, and repeat on the other side. Alternating, work up to 3 sets of 15 per side.

Level
· Advanced

Duration
· 4 minutes

Benefits
· Strengthens core
· Streamlines and defines abdominals and obliques

Caution
· Lower-back issues
· Shoulder issues

Annotation Key
Bold text indicates target muscles
Black text indicates other working muscles
* indicates deep muscles

triceps brachii

deltoideus anterior

rectus abdominis

obliquus externus

serratus anterior

obliquus internus*

transversus abdominis*

Good Mornings

Good Mornings are effective moves for strengthening your lower back. Weight lifters commonly use a barbell to perform Good Mornings, but here your own body weight provides the resistance for the exercise.

1 Stand with your hands clasped behind your head, elbows flared out, and feet shoulder-width apart.

2 Bend your knees slightly and hinge forward from the hips until your back is nearly parallel to the floor.

3 Return to an upright position and repeat, working up to 3 sets of 15 repetitions.

Correct form
· Perform the exercise slowly and with control.

Avoid
· Rounding your back.

Annotation Key
Bold text indicates target muscles
Black text indicates other working muscles
* indicates deep muscles

Level
· Intermediate

Duration
· 3 minutes

Benefits
· Strengthens lower back
· Stretches hamstrings and glutes

Caution
· Lower-back issues

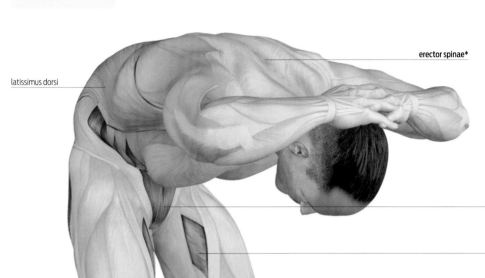

erector spinae*

latissimus dorsi

transversus abdominis*

adductor magnus

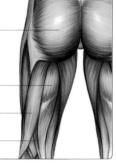

Back View

gluteus maximus

semitendinosus

biceps femoris

semimembranosus

Front View

obliquus internus*

rectus abdominis

obliquus externus

Superman

Superman engages just about every muscle in your body, but it is especially effective at stretching and strengthening the hip flexors. It is also an effective exercise for your back, strengthening both the full extent of the erector spinae, as well as the multifidus spinae. Beware though—this move is harder than it looks.

1 Lie facedown on your stomach with your arms and legs extended on the floor.

2 Raise your arms and your legs simultaneously, squeezing your glutes at the top.

Correct form
· Raise your arms and legs as high as possible.

Avoid
· Overstressing your neck.

3 Lower, and then repeat, working up to 3 sets of 15.

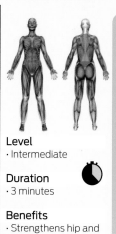

Back View

- semispinalis*
- splenius*
- trapezius
- infraspinatus*
- teres minor
- teres major
- **rhomboideus***
- latissimus dorsi
- **erector spinae***
- quadratus lumborum*

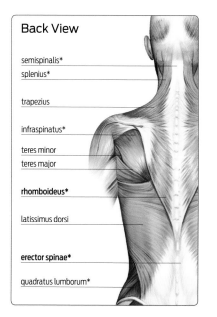

Front View

- sternocleidomastoideus
- scalenus*
- deltoideus anterior
- deltoideus medialis
- biceps brachii
- flexor digitorum*
- extensor carpi radialis

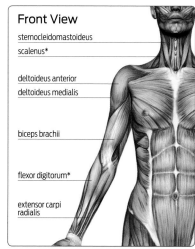

Annotation Key
Bold text indicates target muscles
Black text indicates other working muscles
* indicates deep muscles

Level
· Intermediate

Duration
· 3 minutes

Benefits
· Strengthens hip and spine extensors

Caution
· Back issues

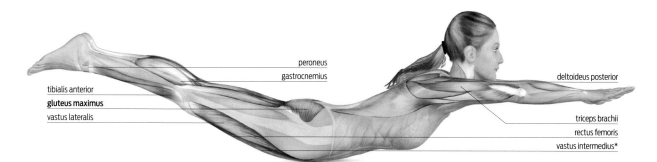

- peroneus
- gastrocnemius
- tibialis anterior
- **gluteus maximus**
- vastus lateralis
- deltoideus posterior
- triceps brachii
- rectus femoris
- vastus intermedius*

Back View

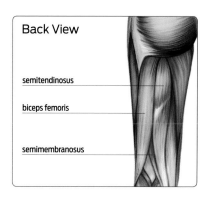

- semitendinosus
- biceps femoris
- semimembranosus

Contents

Back Arch Stretch 160

Child's Pose 161

Fitness Ball
Abdominal Stretch 162

At the end of a long workout session, your body deserves a great cool-down. The cool-down is your time to reflect on your workout, in the process stretching those muscles that have been strengthened, lengthened, tightened, and toned. After pushing yourself to perform numerous repetitions, to work harder, lift heavier, and balance longer, take the time to let your muscles recover. This is where, for instance, the Back Arch Stretch and Fitness Ball Abdominal Stretch, not to mention the ultra-rejuvenating Child's Pose, come in. More than mere relaxation, these stretches help to lock in the progress you've made throughout your workout.

Cool-downs

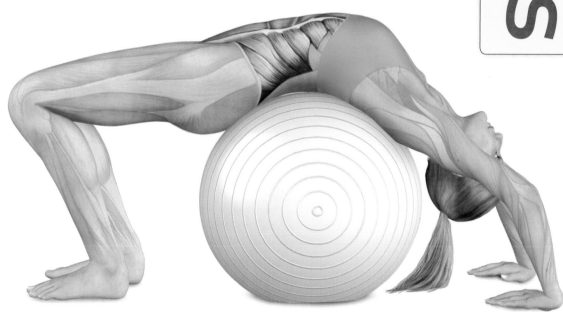

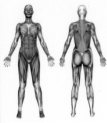

Back Arch Stretch

Back Arch Stretch is an excellent back cool-down exercise. At the end of a long core-training workout, it offers a great stretch for the muscles of your upper and lower back.

Level
· Beginner

Duration
· 1 minute

Benefits
· Stretches back

Caution
· Wrist pain

Correct form
· Keep your abdominals tucked.

Avoid
· Stressing your lower-back muscles by using them to drive the movement.

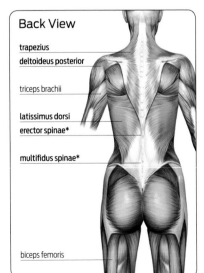

1 Kneel on all fours, with your palms planted hip-distance apart and your knees directly below your hips.

2 Suck in your stomach, imagining it touching the back of your diaphragm.

3 Raise your back as high as you can. Hold this position for 30 seconds.

4 Release, and then repeat for an additional 30 seconds.

Back View

trapezius
deltoideus posterior

triceps brachii

latissimus dorsi
erector spinae*

multifidus spinae*

biceps femoris

Front View

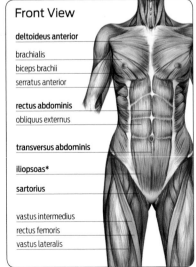

deltoideus anterior

brachialis
biceps brachii
serratus anterior

rectus abdominis
obliquus externus

transversus abdominis

iliopsoas*

sartorius

vastus intermedius
rectus femoris
vastus lateralis

Annotation Key
Bold text indicates target muscles
Black text indicates other working muscles
* indicates deep muscles

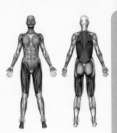

Child's Pose

Child's Pose will effectively stretch your entire back. You can come into this pose at the end of a workout—or at any point in your core-training regimen where you need to rest and reinvigorate your body and mind.

Correct form
· Keep your torso straight.

Avoid
· Hyperextending your lower back.
· Twisting your torso.

Level
· Beginner

Duration
· 1 minute

Benefits
· Stretches back

Caution
· Knee injury

1 Begin facedown with your legs bent, your thighs near your chest and your arms outstretched in front of you.

2 Lean your weight back onto your hips, and elongate your arms as far you can reach. Hold for 30 seconds.

3 Release, and then repeat for an additional 30 seconds.

Annotation Key
Bold text indicates target muscles
Black text indicates other working muscles
* indicates deep muscles

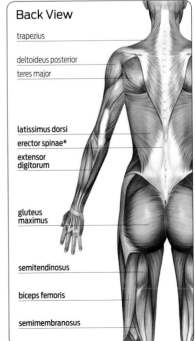

Back View

trapezius
deltoideus posterior
teres major
latissimus dorsi
erector spinae*
extensor digitorum
gluteus maximus
semitendinosus
biceps femoris
semimembranosus

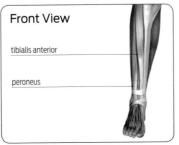

Front View
tibialis anterior
peroneus

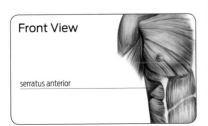

Front View
serratus anterior

Fitness Ball Abdominal Stretch

Fitness Ball Abdominal Stretch makes use of the ball to optimize its impact on your abs. In particular, this stretch benefits your rectus abdominis.

1 Begin on your back on top of a fitness ball, with your feet planted shoulder-width apart and your arms bent, hands beside your head.

Correct form
· Ensure that your entire back remains supported by the ball.
· Anchor your feet to the floor.
· Maintain your body position as you reach backward.

Avoid
· Raising your pelvis excessively high.
· Allowing the ball to wobble.

2 Reach your arms backward until your palms are on the floor.

3 Lower your hips and stretch your pelvis toward the ceiling. Hold for 30 seconds.

4 Release, and then repeat for an additional 30 seconds.

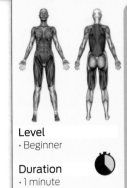

Back View

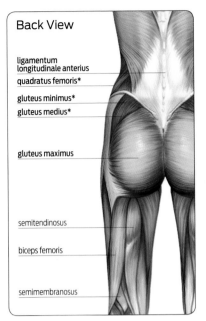

ligamentum
longitudinale anterius
quadratus femoris*
gluteus minimus*
gluteus medius*

gluteus maximus

semitendinosus

biceps femoris

semimembranosus

Front View

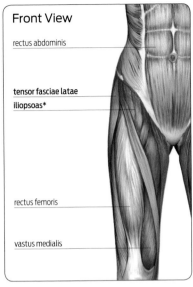

rectus abdominis

tensor fasciae latae
iliopsoas*

rectus femoris

vastus medialis

Level
· Beginner

Duration
· 1 minute

Benefits
· Stretches
  abdominals

Caution
· Lower-back issues
· Balance issues
· Shoulder issues

Annotation Key
Bold text indicates target muscles
Black text indicates other working muscles
* indicates deep muscles

transversus abdominis*

vastus intermedius*
vastus lateralis

pectoralis major
obliquus externus
serratus anterior
pectoralis minor*
latissimus dorsi

deltoideus medialis

flexor carpi radialis

Workouts

Contents

Beginner's Workout 166

Over-Fifty Workout 166

Upper-Abdominal Workout . . .168

Lower-Abdominal Workout . . .168

Global Workout 170

Sports Workout 172

Warrior Workout 174

Beach-Bod Bikini Workout 176

Balance and
Postural Workout 176

Power Workout 178

You have now accumulated a wealth of information about core training. You've warmed up and cooled down, you've stabilized and strengthened—and, along the way, you've picked up an inkling of which exercises will work for you. The following workouts will help you to make core training a way of life. Addressing a range of different needs—from beginner to advanced, upper abs to lower abs, and much more—there is likely to be a workout or two that works for you. Once you get comfortable with these workouts, try making them even more challenging by adding more repetitions, additional exercises, or longer holds. With the knowledge you've gained you can tailor your workout to fit you to a T. When it comes to stabilizing and strengthening your powerhouse, the most effective results come from challenging yourself more and more, every single day.

Beginner's Workout

The Beginner's Workout is a great introduction to core training, and with simple adjustments to the number of sets and repetitions it's suitable for exercisers of all levels.

1 **Plank**
pages 30–31

2 **Fire Hydrant In-Out** pages 40–41

10 **Leg Raise**
pages 142–143

9 **Good Mornings**
pages 154–155

8 **Reverse Crunch**
pages 118–119

Over-Fifty Workout

Core training knows no age limits, and this workout is particularly suited to mature exercisers just embarking on a fitness regime—or anyone looking for a balanced sequence of low-impact moves.

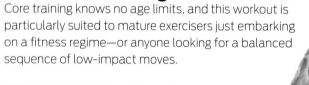

1 **Fitness Ball Hyperextension** pages 54–55

2 **Fitness Ball Bridge**
pages 90–91

10 **Bicycle Crunch**
pages 108–109

9 **Fitness Ball Rollout**
pages 52–53

8 **Fitness Ball Seated Russian Twist** pages 136–137

3 **Fitness Ball Rollout**
pages 52–53

4 **Fitness Ball
Hyperextension** pages 54–55

5 **Hip Crossover**
pages 84–85

7 **Crunch**
pages 106-107

6 **Sit-Up**
pages 98-99

3 **Rise and Reach**
pages 100–101

4 **Penguin Crunch**
pages 128–129

5 **Reverse Crunch**
pages 118–119

7 **Hip Crossover**
pages 84–85

6 **Leg Raise**
pages 142–143

Upper-Abdominal Workout

This workout strengthens and defines the upper abs, helping you to achieve the "six-pack" look.

1 Plank-Up
pages 32–33

2 T-Stabilization
pages 42–43

3 Mountain Climber
pages 56–57

10 Medicine Ball Standing
Russian Twist pages 134–135

9 Wood Chop with Fitness
Ball pages 132–133

Lower-Abdominal Workout

Targeting the hard-to-reach transversus abdominis, this workout will strengthen and tone your lower abdominal muscles.

1 Side Plank
pages 34–35

2 Fire Hydrant
In-Out pages 40–41

3 T-Stabilization
pages 42–43

10 Fitness Ball Russian
Twist pages 138–139

9 Superman
pages 156–157

4 Sit-Up
pages 98–99

5 One-Armed Sit-Up
pages 102–103

6 Crunch
pages 106-107

8 Penguin Crunch
pages 128–129

7 V-Up
pages 114–115

4 Hip Crossover
pages 84–85

5 Hip Raise
pages 86–87

6 Reverse Crunch
pages 118–119

8 Leg Raise
pages 142–143

7 Good Mornings
pages 154–155

Global Workout

Featuring a balanced mix of core stabilizing and strengthening exercises, this workout offers the best of both worlds.

1 Side Plank
pages 34–35

2 Side Plank with Band Row pages 38–39

3 T-Stabilization
pages 42–43

10 One-Armed Sit-Up
pages 102–103

9 Hip Crossover
pages 84–85

11 V-Up
pages 114–115

12 Reverse Crunch
pages 118–119

13 Penguin Crunch
pages 128–129

20 Kneel on Ball
pages 64–65

19 Side Bend
pages 148–149

4 Fitness Ball Rollout
pages 52–53

5 Fitness Ball
Hyperextension pages 54–55

6 Fitness Ball
Band Fly pages 76–77

8 Standing One-Legged
Row pages 94–95

7 Stiff-Legged Deadlift
pages 92–93

14 Leg Raise
pages 142–143

15 Plank-Up
pages 32–33

16 Fitness Ball Jackknife
pages 48–49

18 Medicine Ball Walkover
pages 74–75

17 Fitness Ball
Lateral Roll pages 50–51

Sports Workout

This challenging workout gears up your
core for the rotational performance that
many sports demand.

1 **Plank-Up**
pages 32–33

2 **Side Plank**
pages 34–35

8 **Wood Chop with Fitness
Ball** pages 132–133

7 **V-Up**
pages 114–115

9 **Fitness Ball Seated
Russian Twist** pages 136–137

10 **Fitness Ball Russian
Twist** pages 138–139

11 **Fitness Ball
Split Squat** pages 68–69

16 **Diagonal Crunch with
Medicine Ball** pages 110–111

15 **Medicine Ball
Slam** pages 122–123

3 **T-Stabilization**
pages 42–43

4 **Fitness Ball Atomic
Push-Up** pages 44–45

6 **Mountain Climber**
pages 56–57

5 **Fitness Ball Rollout**
pages 52–53

12 **Fitness Ball Walk-
Around** pages 78–79

13 **Side Lunge and
Press** pages 82–83

14 **Body Saw**
pages 146–147

Warrior Workout

A demanding workout that challenges the
insatiable diehard to maximize core stability,
strength, athleticism, and abdominal visibility.

1 Plank-Up
pages 32–33

2 T-Stabilization
pages 42–43

**9 Fitness Ball Seated
Russian Twist** pages 136–137

8 Penguin Crunch
pages 128–129

10 Leg Raises
pages 142–143

11 Plank
pages 30–31

12 Superman
pages 156–157

**19 Fitness Ball Prone Row to
External Rotation** pages 70–71

18 Fitness Ball Hip Raise
pages 88–89

3 Fitness Ball
Atomic Pushup pages 44–45

4 Body-Weight Squat
pages 58–59

5 Medicine Ball Sit-Up
pages 104–105

7 V-Up
pages 114–115

6 One-Armed Sit-
Up pages 102–103

13 Body Saw
pages 146–147

14 Kneel on Ball
pages 64–65

15 Medicine-Ball
Slam pages 122–123

17 Medicine Ball Pullover
on Fitness Ball pages 80–81

16 Diagonal Crunch with
Medicine Ball pages 110–111

Beach-Bod Bikini Workout

The perfect blend of core exercises—read ripped and defined abs for the beach season, while preparing women to show off a slim waist and trim tummy.

1 Crunch
pages 106–107

2 Bicycle Crunch
pages 108–109

3 V-Up
pages 114–115

13 Side Plank with
Reach-Under pages 36–37

12 Plank
pages 30–31

11 Body Saw
pages 146–147

Balance and Postural Workout

Perform this workout regularly to strengthen both the major and minor muscles that assist your posture and balance.

1 Medicine Ball Squat
to Press pages 60–61

2 Medicine Ball Walkover
pages 74–75

6 T-Stabilization
pages 42–43

4 **One-Armed Sit-Up** pages 102–103

5 **Vertical Leg Crunch** pages 150–151

6 **Reverse Crunch** pages 118–119

7 **Band Roll-Down with Twist** pages 152–153

10 **Fitness Ball Alternating Leg Tuck** pages 140–141

9 **Leg Raise** pages 142–143

8 **Penguin Crunch** pages 128–129

3 **Balance Push-Up** pages 62–63

5 **Fitness Ball Seated External Rotation** pages 72–73

4 **Fitness Ball Prone Row to External Rotation** pages 70–71

Power Workout

This strenuous workout will build core strength, allowing you to power through whatever physical challenges come your way.

1 Big Circles with
Medicine Ball pages 120–121

2 Medicine-Ball
Slam pages 122–123

3 Diagonal Crunch with
Medicine Ball pages 110–111

10 Fitness Ball Seated
Russian Twist pages 136–137

9 Wood Chop with Band
pages 130–131

11 Kneel on Ball
pages 64–65

12 Side Lunge and
Press pages 82–83

18 Side Plank with
Band Row pages 38–39

17 Side Plank with Reach-
Under pages 36–37

4 **Fitness Ball Atomic Push-Up** pages 44–45

5 **Fitness Ball Jackknife** pages 48–49

6 **Fitness Ball Pike** pages 46–47

8 **Fitness Ball Crunch** pages 116–117

7 **Fitness Ball Side Crunch** pages 112–113

13 **Medicine Ball Over-the-Shoulder Throw** pages 66–67

14 **Fitness Ball Walk-Around** pages 78–79

16 **Kneeling Crunch with Band** pages 124–125

15 **Fitness Ball Split Squat** pages 68–69

Conclusion

Congratulations! You've now learned how to perform a wide range of dynamic, challenging, and multifaceted exercises. Equipped with the tools in this book, you have all you need to both stabilize and strengthen those all-important core muscles, which you rely on every single day.

So what comes next?

It's now time to make core training a regular part of your life. You can join a health club, but if you have a corner of the living room, some workout clothes, and perhaps a mat, then your home gym is complete. And through exploring this book, you have learned all about what your core muscles do and how to work them most effectively. The rest is up to you.

Don't be limited by the workouts shown here. After grasping the basics of core training, and exploring an array of exercises, try creating your own fitness routines based on your needs. However you choose to incorporate core training into your daily life, don't forget: in setting aside time to work your core, you're moving further down the path to a fitter, leaner, better-functioning, stronger physique.

Websites

Because of the changing nature of Internet links, Rosen Publishing has developed an online list of websites related to the subject of this book. This site is updated regularly. Please use this link to access the list:

http://www.rosenlinks.com/FMB/Core

Glossary

GENERAL TERMINOLOGY

abduction: Movement away from the body.

adduction: Movement toward the body.

anterior: Located in the front.

cardiovascular exercise: Any exercise that increases the heart rate, making oxygen and nutrient-rich blood available to working muscles.

cervical spine: The upper area of the spine immediately below the skull.

cool-down: An exercise performed at the end of the workout session that works to cool and relax the body after more vigorous exertion.

core stabilizer: An exercise that calls for resisting motion at the lumbar spine though activation of the abdominal muscles and deep stabilizers; improves core strength and endurance.

core strengthener: An exercise that allows for motion in the lumbar spine, while working the abdominal muscles and deep stabilizers; improves movement such as running or walking.

core: Refers to the deep muscle layers that lie close to the spine and provide structural support for the entire body. The core is divisible into two groups: major core and minor core muscles. Major muscles reside on the trunk and include the belly area and the mid and lower back. This area encompasses the pelvic floor muscles (levator ani, pubococcygeus, iliococcygeus, pubo-rectalis, and coccygeus), the abdominals (rectus abdominis, transversus abdominis, obliquus externus, and obliquus internus), the spinal extensors (multifidus spinae, erector spinae, splenius, longissimus thoracis, and semispinalis), and the diaphragm. The minor core includes the latissimus dorsi, gluteus maximus, and trapezius (upper, middle, and lower). Minor core muscles assist the major muscles when the body engages in activities or movements that require added stability.

crunch: A common abdominal exercise that calls for curling the shoulders toward the pelvis while lying supine with hands behind head and knees bent.

deadlift: An exercise movement that calls for lifting a weight, such as a barbell, off the ground from a stabilized bent-over position.

dumbbell: A basic piece of resistance equipment that consists of a short bar on which plates are secured. A person can use a dumbbell in one hand or both hands during an exercise.

exercise mat: A firm mat, usually made of foam rubber, that is at least one-half inch (1.27 cm) thick. The roll-up variety typically measures about 72 to 86 inches (180–220 cm), with widths varying from 20 or so inches to close to 40 inches (50–100 cm).

extension: The act of straightening.

extensor muscle: A muscle serving to extend a body part away from the center of the body.

external rotation: The act of moving a body part away from the center of the body.

fitness ball: A large, inflatable ball sometimes used for support during a core-training workout. It brings the core muscles into play, using them for balance and stability. Also called a Swiss ball.

flexion: The bending of a joint.

flexor muscle: A muscle that decreases the angle between two bones, as bending the arm at the elbow or raising the thigh toward the stomach.

fly: An exercise movement in which the hand and arm move through an arc while the elbow is kept at a constant angle. Fly exercises work the muscles of the upper body.

hand weights: Small weights that can be incorporated into Pilates exercises to enhance strengthening and toning benefits.

hyperextension: An exercise that works the lower back as well as the mid and upper back, specifically the erector spinae, which usually involves raising the torso and/or lower body from the floor while keeping the pelvis firmly anchored.

iliotibial band (ITB): A thick band of fibrous tissue that runs down the outside of the leg, beginning at the hip and extending to the outer side of the tibia just below the knee joint. The band functions in concert with several of the thigh muscles to provide stability to the outside of the knee joint.

internal rotation: The act of moving a body part toward the center of the body.

isometric exercise: A form of exercise involving the static contraction of a muscle without any visible movement in the angle of the joint.

lateral: Located on, or extending toward, the outside.

lumbar spine: The lower part of the spine.

medial: Located on, or extending toward, the middle.

medicine ball: A small weighted ball used in weight training and toning.

neutral position: A position in which the natural curve of the spine is maintained, typically adopted when lying on one's back with one or both feet on the mat.

neutral: Describes the position of the legs, pelvis, hips, or other part of the body that is neither arched nor curved forward.

plate: A cast-iron weight placed on a dumbbell. The weight of plates generally start at a 1¼ pounds (.56 kg) and range upward to 50 pounds (22 kg) and higher.

posterior: Located behind.

press: An exercise movement that calls for moving a weight or other resistance away from the body.

range of motion: The distance and direction a joint can move between the flexed position and the extended position.

resistance band: Any rubber tubing or flat band device that provides a resistive force used for strength training. Also called a "fitness band," "stretching band," and "stretch tube."

rotator muscle: One of a group of muscles that assists the rotation of a joint, such as the hip or the shoulder.

scapula: The protrusion of bone on the mid to upper back, also known as the "shoulder blade."

split squat: An assisted one-legged squat where the nonlifting leg is rested on the floor a few steps behind the lifting leg, as if it were a static lunge.

squat: An exercise movement that calls for moving the hips back and bending the knees and hips to lower the torso and an accompanying weight, and then returning to the upright position. A squat primarily targets the muscles of the thighs, hips, buttocks, and hamstrings.

synergistic exercise: Combinations of exercises or diet and exercise strategically used to produce optimal results in the least amount of time.

thoracic spine: The middle part of the spine.

warm-up: Any form of light exercise of short duration that prepares the body for more intense exercise.

LATIN TERMINOLOGY

The following glossary list explains the Latin terminology used to describe the body's musculature. In some instances, certain words are derived from Greek, which is therein indicated.

Chest

coracobrachialis: Greek *korakoeidés*, "ravenlike," and *brachium*, "arm"

pectoralis (major and minor): *pectus*, "breast"

Abdomen

obliquus externus: *obliquus*, "slanting," and *externus*, "outward"

obliquus internus: *obliquus*, "slanting," and *internus*, "within"

rectus abdominis: *rego*, "straight, upright," and *abdomen*, "belly"

serratus anterior: *serra*, "saw," and *ante*, "before"

transversus abdominis: *transversus*, "athwart," and *abdomen*, "belly"

Neck

scalenus: Greek *skalénós*, "unequal"

semispinalis: *semi*, "half," and *spinae*, "spine"

splenius: Greek *spléníon*, "plaster, patch"

sternocleidomastoideus: Greek *stérnon*, "chest," Greek *kleís*, "key," and Greek *mastoeidés*, "breastlike"

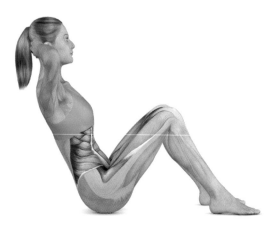

Back

erector spinae: *erectus*, "straight," and *spina*, "thorn"

latissimus dorsi: *latus*, "wide," and *dorsum*, "back"

multifidus spinae: *multifid*, "to cut into divisions," and *spinae*, "spine"

quadratus lumborum: *quadratus*, "square, rectangular," and *lumbus*, "loin"

rhomboideus: Greek *rhembesthai*, "to spin"

trapezius: Greek *trapezion*, "small table"

Shoulders

deltoideus (anterior, medial, and posterior): Greek *deltoeidés*, "delta-shaped"

infraspinatus: *infra*, "under," and *spina*, "thorn"

levator scapulae: *levare*, "to raise," and *scapulae*, "shoulder [blades]"

subscapularis: *sub*, "below," and *scapulae*, "shoulder [blades]"

supraspinatus: *supra*, "above," and *spina*, "thorn"

teres (major and minor): *teres*, "rounded"

Upper arm

biceps brachii: *biceps*, "two-headed," and *brachium*, "arm"

brachialis: *brachium*, "arm"

triceps brachii: *triceps*, "three-headed," and *brachium*, "arm"

Lower arm

anconeus: Greek *anconad*, "elbow"

brachioradialis: *brachium*, "arm," and *radius*, "spoke"

extensor carpi radialis: *extendere*, "to extend," Greek *karpós*, "wrist," and *radius*, "spoke"

extensor digitorum: *extendere*, "to extend," and *digitus*, "finger, toe"

flexor carpi pollicis longus: *flectere*, "to bend," Greek *karpós*, "wrist," *pollicis*, "thumb," and *longus*, "long"

flexor carpi radialis: *flectere*, "to bend," Greek *karpós*, "wrist," and *radius*, "spoke"

flexor carpi ulnaris: *flectere*, "to bend," Greek *karpós*, "wrist," and *ulnaris*, "forearm"

flexor digitorum: *flectere*, "to bend," and *digitus*, "finger, toe"

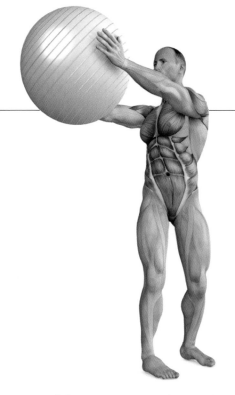

palmaris longus: *palmaris*, "palm," and *longus*, "long"

pronator teres: *pronate*, "to rotate," and *teres*, "rounded"

Hips

gemellus (inferior and superior): *geminus*, "twin"

gluteus maximus: Greek *gloutós*, "rump," and *maximus*, "largest"

gluteus medius: Greek *gloutós*, "rump," and *medialis*, "middle"

gluteus minimus: Greek *gloutós*, "rump," and *minimus*, "smallest"

iliopsoas: *ilium*, "groin," and Greek *psoa*, "groin muscle"

iliacus: *ilium*, "groin"

obturator externus: *obturare*, "to block," and *externus*, "outward"

obturator internus: *obturare*, "to block," and *internus*, "within"

pectineus: *pectin*, "comb"

piriformis: *pirum*, "pear," and *forma*, "shape"

quadratus femoris: *quadratus*, "square, rectangular," and *femur*, "thigh"

Upper leg

adductor longus: *adducere*, "to contract," and *longus*, "long"

adductor magnus: *adducere*, "to contract," and *magnus*, "major"

biceps femoris: *biceps*, "two-headed," and *femur*, "thigh"

gracilis: *gracilis*, "slim, slender"

rectus femoris: *rego*, "straight, upright," and *femur*, "thigh"

sartorius: *sarcio*, "to patch" or "to repair"

semimembranosus: *semi*, "half," and *membrum*, "limb"

semitendinosus: *semi*, "half," and *tendo*, "tendon"

tensor fasciae latae: *tenere*, "to stretch," *fasciae*, "band," and *latae*, "laid down"

vastus intermedius: *vastus*, "immense, huge," and *intermedius*, "between"

vastus lateralis: *vastus*, "immense, huge," and *lateralis*, "side"

vastus medialis: *vastus*, "immense, huge," and *medialis*, "middle"

Lower leg

adductor digiti minimi: *adducere*, "to contract," *digitus*, "finger, toe," and *minimum*, "smallest"

adductor hallucis: *adducere*, "to contract," and *hallex*, "big toe"

extensor digitorum: *extendere*, "to extend," and *digitus*, "finger, toe"

extensor hallucis: *extendere*, "to extend," and *hallex*, "big toe"

flexor digitorum: *flectere*, "to bend," and *digitus*, "finger, toe"

flexor hallucis: *flectere*, "to bend," and *hallex*, "big toe"

gastrocnemius: Greek *gastroknémía*, "calf [of the leg]"

peroneus: *peronei*, "of the fibula"

plantaris: *planta*, "the sole"

soleus: *solea*, "sandal"

tibialis anterior: *tibia*, "reed pipe," and *ante*, "before"

tibialis posterior: *tibia*, "reed pipe," and *posterus*, "coming after"

Icon Index

Supine Lower-Back Stretch
page 24

Side Stretch
page 25

Half-Kneeling Rotation
page 26

Plank
page 30

Plank-Up
page 32

Side Plank
page 34

Side Plank with Reach-Under
page 36

Side Plank with Band Row
page 38

Fire-Hydrant In-Out
page 40

T-Stabilization
page 42

Fitness Ball Atomic Push-Up
page 44

Fitness Ball Pike
page 46

Fitness Ball Jackknife
page 48

Fitness Ball Lateral Roll
page 50

Fitness Ball Rollout
page 52

Fitness Ball Hyperextension
page 54

Mountain Climber
page 56

Body-Weight Squat
page 58

Medicine Ball Squat to Press
page 60

Balance Push-Up
page 62

Kneel on Ball
page 64

Med. Ball Over-the-Shoulder Throw
page 66

Fitness Ball Split Squat
page 68

Fitness Ball Prone Row Ext. Rotation
page 70

Fitness Ball Seated Ext. Rotation
page 72

Medicine Ball Walkover
page 74

Fitness Ball Band Fly
page 76

Fitness Ball Walk-Around
page 78

Med. Ball Pullover on Fitness Ball
page 80

Side Lunge and Press
page 82

Hip Crossover
page 84

Hip Raise
page 86

Fitness Ball Hip Raise
page 88

Fitness Ball Bridge
page 90

Stiff-Legged Deadlift
page 92

Standing One-Legged Row
page 94

Sit-Up
page 98

Rise and Reach
page 100

One-Armed Sit-Up
page 102

Medicine Ball Sit-Up
page 104

Crunch
page 106

Bicycle Crunch
page 108

Diagonal Crunch with Med. Ball
page 110

Fitness Ball Side Crunch
page 112

V-Up
page 114

Fitness Ball Crunch
page 116

Reverse Crunch
page 118

Big Circles with Medicine Ball
page 120

Medicine Ball Slam
page 122

Kneeling Crunch with Band
page 124

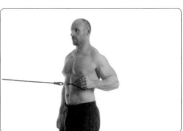

One-Armed Band Pull
page 126

Penguin Crunch
page 128

Wood Chop with Band
page 130

Wood Chop with Fitness Ball
page 132

Med. Ball Standing Russian Twist
page 134

Fitness Ball Seated Russian Twist
page 136

Fitness Ball Russian Twist
page 138

Fitness Ball Alternating Leg Tuck
page 140

Leg Raise
page 142

Side Leg Raise
page 144

Body Saw
page 146

Side Bend
page 148

Vertical Leg Crunch
page 150

Band Roll-Down with Twist
page 152

Good Mornings
page 154

Superman
page 156

Back Arch Stretch
page 160

Child's Pose
page 161

Fitness Ball Abdominal Stretch
page 162

About the author

Hollis Lance Liebman has been a fitness magazine editor and national bodybuilding champion. He is a published physique photographer and has served as a bodybuilding and fitness competition judge. Currently a Los Angeles resident, Hollis has worked with some of Hollywood's elite, earning rave reviews. Visit his Web site, www.holliswashere.com, for fitness tips and complete training programs.

Core-training model Cori D. Cohen is a registered dietitian and healthy lifestyle coach based in New York City. She provides private nutrition counseling to a diverse clientele, in addition to working with residents at a nursing and rehabilitation center. Ms. Cohen has degrees from the University of Delaware, Fashion Institute of Technology, CUNY Queens College, and LIU C. W. Post. She is currently featured as a columnist for the *Queens Courier*, where she provides readers with valuable nutrition advice.

Credits

All photographs by Jonathan Conklin Photography, Inc. (jonathanconklin. net), except for the following:

Page 8 Paul Cotney/Shutterstock.com; page 11 AVAVA/Shutterstock. com; page 13 Lana K/Shutterstock.com; page 14 top Africa Studio/ Shutterstock.com; page 14 bottom StockLite/Shutterstock.com; page 16 Beth Van Trees/Shutterstock.com; page 17 bottom left Valeriy Lebedev/ Shutterstock.com; page 17 top left Olga Miltsova/Shutterstock.com; page 17 middle Viktor1/Shutterstock.com; page 17 bottom PHB.cz (Richard Semik)/Shutterstock.com; page 18 top left Africa Studio/Shutterstock. com; page 18 bottom left Nattika/Shutterstock.com; page 18 bottom middle joingate/Shutterstock.com; page 18 bottom right Aleksandr Stennikov/Shutterstock.com; page 19 top Liliia Rudchenko/Shutterstock. com; page 19 middle Juice Team/Shutterstock.com; page 19 bottom Valentyn Volkov/Shutterstock.com; pages 180–181 Kzenon/Shutterstock. com; page 192 left Sonia Keshishian.

All anatomical illustrations by Hector Aiza/3D Labz Animation India (www.3dlabz.com), except small insets and full-body anatomy on pages 20–21 by Linda Bucklin/Shutterstock.com, and page 9 sam100/ Shutterstock.com.